MW00904335

ONLY GOD CAN MAKE A BUTTERFLY

Transforming Our Nature, Our Nation and Our Notion of Religion One Caterpillar at a Time

David J. Delnostro, M.D.

www.xulonpress.com

Table of Contents

/

Acknowledgements

The time and effort it took to write *Only God Can Make a Butterfly* rivaled that of my medical training. However, unlike medical school, many people helped me along the way. My wife, Beth, encouraged me to put my ideas into a book. She and I spent many hours discussing and analyzing my psychological concepts and Biblical interpretations. In the two years it took me to finish this project, we had our share of share of disagreements. Beth has the communication degree, while I only have a medical degree. It is one thing to be able to analyze and conceptualize, it is another to be able to describe it in easily understandable terms. Sometimes, when I expected her to give me a pat on the head for a job well done, she gave me a gentle kick in the behind to make it better. Although I did not appreciate it then, I am grateful to her now for not letting me settle for mediocrity. She has also done a wonderful job designing the front cover.

I am blessed with many friends and neighbors, who sacrificed their time to read my document at various stages of production and shared their thoughts and impressions with me. I am especially grateful to my friends, Forrest Williams and Jim Scheidel, who spent hours reading and critiquing my book several times at different stages of completion. I greatly appreciate their input and encouragement.

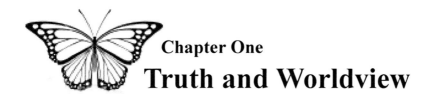

Chapter One
Truth and Worldview

"But when He, the Spirit of truth, comes, He will guide you into all the truth; for He will not speak on His own initiative, but whatever He hears, He will speak; and He will disclose to you what is to come.
John 16:13 NASB

"Christianity is the only true and perfect religion, and that in proportion as mankind adopts its principles and obeys its precepts, they will be wise and happy."
Benjamin Rush -Signer Declaration of Independence,

Life is full of complex and confounding questions!

Why are some people takers and others givers? What causes one person to be depressed and anxious while the another person in the same situation is merely concerned and remains hopeful? Why does one husband stay true to his wife, while the other one strays? What makes one person insecure and a people-pleaser while the other is bold and self-confident? Why does one man acknowledge there is evil in the world and another does not?

Have you ever wondered why college professors and students tend to be liberals? How can some Catholics, Jews and Christians become liberal while others are conservative? How can one woman see abortion as a right, while the other sees it as murder? What do socialists and Muslims have in common? Why do Americans see the role of government and our Constitution differently? How can two different groups of human beings, who have normally functioning brains, behave so differently?

The answer to all of these questions is **worldview**, which I define as the perspective from which a person perceives himself, his fellow man, and the world around him. It is my contention that we only have two worldviews available to us. Unfortunately, our two worldviews — the two interpretations of reality — can not both be correct. The incorrect worldview leads us to base our beliefs on a false understanding of the human condition. The correct worldview leads us to base our beliefs on the true understanding of our world and our role in it.

In the course of discussing the two worldviews available to us, I will address the following questions:

- Is it possible for human beings to determine which worldview is correct so we can base our lives on the truth, or do we have to know the truth so we can have the correct worldview? In other words, which comes first, the chicken or the egg?

- Are we able to determine the proper perspective from which we can attain this new worldview? And, if we do not currently possess the correct perspective, can we change it?

- Do humans undergo a transformation similar to a caterpillar's metamorphosis into a butterfly? And, if we do, will we see one worldview as the truth and then be transformed? Or, must we be transformed so we can know which worldview is true?

- Finally, if we want to be transformed, can we do it by ourselves or do we need help? And, if we do need help, who will be our helper?

Once these questions are answered, we will be able to distinguish the correct worldview from the incorrect one, thus allowing us to recognize the truth from a lie!

Common sense tells us that living according to a false version of reality will result in living dysfunctional, sub-optimal lives. Conversely, living according to the truth will allow us to live our most functional and meaningful lives. Since knowing the truth plays an integral role in our ability to live in an effective and functional manner, I would like to spend a few moments discussing the meaning of the word "truth".

Consider the following scenario. A person is summoned to testify as a witness in a murder trial. When he is sworn in, he is asked to tell the truth, the whole truth, and nothing but the truth. Have you ever thought about what that truly means? The judge wants him to tell the "truth" from his perspective. If he witnessed a murder, he can only testify to what he observed from his particular vantage point. Telling the "whole truth" means not leaving anything out of his narrative for any reason. "Nothing but the truth" means he is not to guess, extrapolate, embellish, or surmise to fill in the gaps in his testimony. If he is honest in his recollection, the judge and jury will hear his best version of the truth. **This means "the truth, the whole truth, and nothing but the truth" is the best truth man can know.** However, it is not the absolute truth regarding the crime because it can only be seen from one perspective, and man's observations are limited to his senses and subject to his individual interpretation.

Therefore, the absolute truth can only be known if the person witnessed the murder from every vantage point. This means he had to view the crime from every perspective including from inside the body and mind of the victim and the murderer. He would have had to be present for the entire duration of the crime without missing a detail on the part of every participant. This kind of truth is like a video of the crime from every vantage point with every thought from each person combined and integrated into a single story. All the testimony would have to come from a witness with perfect recall and whose life experiences and emotional state of mind would not influence his account of the details of the event.

The absolute truth can never be known by human beings, regardless of the number of people who witnessed the murder. The absolute truth can only be known by a living being who can view events from all perspectives and from beginning to end, as if he were observing from outside of time. The only being who fits this description is God. Only God can know the absolute truth. In mathematical terms, the difference between God's absolute truth and man's truth is the remainder of the truth; the unknown truth. When man tries to determine the unknown truth, he will usually fill in the gaps with his best estimate. This guess is influenced by his upbringing, personal traumas, life experiences, information and misinformation from his parents and teachers, or from accounts of other people or books he has read. He is psychologically driven to fill in the gaps in a way that makes sense to him. Unfortunately, since man is not perfect, his truth will be partial at best and erroneous at its worst. **A wrong or incomplete truth in God's domain is called a *lie*.**

A man's worldview is the lens through which he observes and interprets himself and the world around him, and it is from that worldview that his psyche develops. Therefore, once we understand the psychology of each of these two worldviews, we can better see the link between a person's worldview and his individual attitudes, values and behaviors. **A person who sees the world from man's perspective will adopt values and morals based on relative truths, which will result in a false understanding of reality. The person who sees the world from God's perspective will adopt values and morals based on absolute truth, which will result in the true understanding of reality.**

Living according to man's worldview leads us to accept relative truths. The problem with relative truths is they are also relative lies, and living according to relative lies causes us to get off track and live sub-optimal and dysfunctional lives. We can only live our most functional lives if we know the absolute truth about ourselves. Only when we live according to God's worldview will the absolute truth begin to be revealed to us. Although God knows all the absolute truths, we can only know the absolute truths God reveals to us. We will never know all that God knows because we are not God.

The absolute truth can only be known from God's perspective. Regardless of his educational level or his life experiences, man can learn many things, but he can never learn the absolute truth about himself and the manner in which to live his life. The absolute truth must be imparted to him by God. No other source of truth is available to us. Only God can tell us the truth about our purpose, worth, and the manner in which we are to live our lives. However, we must come to know God before He will reveal His truths to us.

The benefits of attaining God's worldview are not limited to individuals. Societies that hold the proper worldview will direct their citizens to follow God's moral system and not make one more suitable to themselves. These cultures or countries that see the world from God's perspective will also choose an economic philosophy that is consistent with healthy human psychology. This allows them to function within the common-sense laws of economics. Once societies obtain the correct, most functional perspective from which to operate, they will naturally gravitate to a government system based upon truth. This system will proficiently serve its citizens, yet not grow so large and overbearing that it will control and oppress them.

Since only two worldviews are available to individuals of any society, the predominant worldview of its citizens will determine which worldview is followed. This worldview will determine their morality, which affects their psychological health and well-being. I hope to convince you that we can not expect to heal a person's broken life or fix a social problem without addressing the worldview of the person or persons involved. It would be like treating a starving caterpillar by forcing him to feed on the nectar of flowers rather than leaves. The treatment would not only be doomed to fail, it would inevitably cause the caterpillar's death.

I hope it will become evident, in the course of reading this book, that the best way to improve the lives of human beings is through worldview transformation, not higher education. No matter how educated people become, the knowledge acquired can only be used to better understand their current worldview. **Knowledge can not give a person a new worldview.** People must be transformed in the same way a caterpillar is transformed into a butterfly, so they can develop a new, more functional worldview that will forever change the way they behave and live their lives. When it comes to living the abundant life, changing our worldview can only occur when we are born again as butterflies… and only God can make a butterfly!

The truth is summed up in one Word, and if you are still not sure of the identity of this Word, let me refer you to the Gospel of John. "In the beginning the Word already existed. The Word was with God, and the Word was God. He existed in the beginning with God. God created everything through Him and nothing was created except through Him" (John 1:1-3 NLT). I have written this book because I know the Word and He knows me. The Word is a person and his name is Jesus. He sought me out and found me years ago, and His love for me saved me from the dysfunctional life of a caterpillar and certain death. Over the years, I have learned to love Him back, and it is my love for Him that set the stage for God to transform me into a butterfly.

Once enough of our neighbors in America and around the world are transformed from caterpillars into butterflies, they will have a new worldview and develop a new nature. They will gain the true view of reality, which will help them solve problems that confront them rather than make their lives worse. As more people are transformed, maybe our crazy world will start to make sense again, and I, for one, can stop yelling at the TV.

The Author's Transformation

My transformation occurred when I finally understood that God is God, and I am not! When I accepted this fact, it changed my perspective and determined the way I was to live my life. There was no reason for me to continue to live like a caterpillar once I realized that God could make me into a glorious butterfly. Once I submitted my life to Christ, He took a functional atheist and transformed me into a new creation with spectacular wings large enough to lift me out of my self-centered world. He set me free from being earth-bound and lost in the darkness of the world into which I was born. Before this miraculous transformation, I did not have the perspective to see the absolute truth about my own value and purpose in life. Now, I do. I have finally begun to experience the love that God has been trying to bestow upon me since I was a little larva.

For the past thirteen years, I have done my best to use my new wings to follow Jesus and fly according to His will. As a result of my obedience to God, I am able to experience the world from His perspective, the Biblical perspective. Once God transformed me into a butterfly, He transplanted a new nature into me — His just, generous and loving nature. Not only have I been made in His likeness, I have grown closer to Him to see my true self reflected in His eyes. God loves me and values me as He does His own Divine Son. For the first time, my purpose for living is crystal clear, and the manner in which I am to live my life makes perfect sense to me.

Life for me was not always fulfilling and rewarding. I was born a Jewish caterpillar and stayed a caterpillar for the first forty years of my life. I methodically and successfully crawled and consumed my way through life. No matter how full I became, I felt the emptiness that so many of us larvae feel without God residing in that place within us that is reserved only for Him. Early in my adult life, I had given up on the notion of God, but God never gave up on me. Fortunately, Christ pursued me until I caught Him about a month before my wedding day in 1992. With the guidance of my butterfly bride, I professed my faith in Jesus and was baptized on the day we were married. Sadly, it was not until 1998 that I became a true follower of my Lord, Jesus Christ. My acceptance of Jesus as my Savior allowed me to call myself a Christian, but I remained a caterpillar. I had not yet surrendered my entire life to Him and made Him my Lord, as well. Until I submitted myself into the Creator's hands, He could not begin my transformation into a butterfly. **As I have since learned, there is a vast difference between calling oneself a Christian and becoming a surrendered follower of Christ!** My pastor has said many times that going to church once a week no more makes one a Christian than going to the chicken coup once a week makes one a chicken. In no time at all, my perspective on life began to change, and I started to experience a more positive, peaceful and hopeful outlook on life. My confidence and demeanor started to resemble the more mature Christians in my church and home Bible group.

During the last few years, I have read and studied the Bible, and God has made it clear that mankind possesses a congenitally, sinful nature. It seemed logical to me that if all men possessed a sinful nature, and God was willing to die in order to free us from this nature, there must be another nature available and preferable for man to possess. Jesus did not die to give man a new religion, but to rescue him from one. He came to help man change his perspective on life by making us into new creations with a new nature consistent with His. **Christ did not want to become my God because I was an atheist and did not have a god. He wanted to become my God because I *did* have one, and it was me. He did not want me to spend a lifetime serving a false and inadequate god.**

My new perspective on life formed my overall worldview, which changed my understanding of how the world truly worked and how I fit into it. It was my new worldview that determined my values, my decisions and my behavior. If you follow my logic, this means that our perspective, which determines our worldview and nature, depends on whether we live as our own god the way we were born, or whether we choose to make Jesus our God. Why only Jesus is God, I will explain later in the text of the book.

Human nature can be changed by merely transferring the authority under which we live from ourselves to God. It is a simple concept, but it takes a deep faith and immense courage to die unto oneself and trust God enough to submit to His authority and control. Becoming a follower of Christ is not for chickens!

As a physician, I am in the business of restoring health and saving lives. Over the course of thirty years of practice, I have analyzed my observations of human behavior and discovered the psychological effects each worldview has on the individual. I found that adopting the proper worldview can positively affect our emotional and psychological health. I intend to prove that one worldview is correct, and the other is unequivocally wrong because it adversely affects our overall emotional and psychological well-being. If our worldview is wrong, then our premise for life is wrong. If our premise for life is wrong, the conclusions we make about ourselves and our world will also be wrong. Our dysfunctional choices and behavior will have a grave effect on our individual lives, our families, our government and our culture. **With God's guidance, I have discovered the cure for man's congenital self-centered, caterpillar worldview, which I call "the cancer of human living."** Clearly, it would be malpractice as a physician and a follower of Christ not to share the cure with all of those for whom Jesus died — and that means everyone!

What's in the Book?

Living with God at the controls has been such an eye-opening adventure, I want each of you to experience your own adventure with Him. However, before this can happen, you must be properly introduced to the Truth, who is Jesus. I have written this book in the form of a systematic explanation, offering a logical proof in a slow, methodical, and orderly fashion regarding the role of God in the determination of our worldviews. It also provides a psychological interpretation of the Bible, which confirms that living within the Biblical worldview is the only way for people to achieve optimal mental and emotional health.

Several months ago I submitted a political Letter to the Editor of our local newspaper and received a great deal of positive feedback regarding my caterpillar-butterfly analogy. So, on a rainy day I just started writing. I had already written an unpublished thesis on the *Psychology of Two Worldviews* early in 2009, and I simply added to it. Within this book, I have presented personal commentary on many passages of scripture from my Christian and physician point of view. I am a culture watcher and political junkie, so there is a significant portion devoted to social and political commentary. I am terribly concerned about the direction our political leaders are dragging my beloved America. There is even a short course in entomology, specifically on butterflies.

Mostly, I wrote this book so others could use it as a Christian apologetics handbook. It interprets Biblical scripture primarily from a medical and psychological perspective as well as from a theological one. As a byproduct of showing the importance of worldview, I have presented a logical analysis to prove that while the Bible still remains God's Holy Book, it is primarily a medical textbook and a psychological primer for life. Yes, it catalogs the history of God's interplay and relationship with mankind throughout the ages, but I will demonstrate that it most certainly was not intended to be a religious book.

Only God Can Make a Butterfly represents my prescription for life. It outlines my treatment plan to overcome the pathological emotional, psychological and behavioral consequences that natural-born humans have experienced since they inhabited the Earth. I wrote this in the hope that I could penetrate people's emotional, psychological, intellectual, religious, and cultural barriers regarding Jesus and knock down those walls. My greatest desire is to make it possible for them to escape their own self-centered world. Once this has occurred, they will be able to experience the transforming, life-healing power of our Creator. I wanted to impress upon my fellow human beings that the more they insist on remaining their own masters, the more like slaves they will become. To quote Matthew 10:39 (NIV), "If you give up your life for me, you will find it."

Conversely, if you will not give control of your life to God, you will lose it. A life not surrendered to God represents a misspent life!

I set out to prove that choosing to live under Christ's authority is not a religious choice, but a medical and psychological prerequisite for more proper and effective living. I wanted to make the case that the Biblical Christian worldview is the only functional worldview that it is consistent with the reality in which we live. After many years as a practicing physician, I have dealt with people at their most vulnerable and most joyous moments, and have come to agree with my Pastor, Cam Huxford. People, who live with Jesus at the center of their lives, laugh better, love better, cry better, and die better than those who do not. **I wrote this book to show everyone that life is not about discovering and learning the truth about living. It is about knowing and loving the Truth in the person of Jesus Christ.**

In this book, I will add clarity to the answers of many of life's questions by comparing both worldviews and connecting human psychology with the scriptural truths inscribed in the Holy Bible. However, the most important question must be asked and answered by you. How do you want to travel through life? Crawling all over each other consuming leaf after leaf like a caterpillar or gliding freely from flower to flower in God's light and grace like a beautiful butterfly? It is your choice. Make the right one because the quality of your life on Earth and your chance to experience an eternal one in Heaven depend on it!

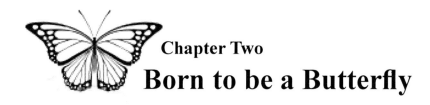

Chapter Two
Born to be a Butterfly

Do not conform any longer to the pattern of this world, but be transformed by the renewing of your mind. Then you will be able to test and approve what God's will is—his good, pleasing and perfect will.

Romans 12:2 NIV.

"It cannot be emphasized too strongly or too often that this great nation was founded, not by religionists, but by Christians; not on religions, but on the Gospel of Jesus Christ...."

Patrick Henry 1776

Many years ago I visited the butterfly conservatory at Callaway Gardens in Pine Mountain, Georgia. It was absolutely breathtaking to be surrounded by so many different kinds of butterflies and their corresponding caterpillars and cocoons. For nearly an hour, I meandered through this glass-enclosed garden and observed the differences between each butterfly and their larval caterpillar counterpart. It is difficult to believe that, although they appeared to be entirely unrelated creatures and lived their lives so differently, they shared the same DNA. The creepy caterpillars crawled all over each other and lived their lives viewing the garden from the ground up. The butterflies flew effortlessly and viewed the garden from above. Caterpillars fed on leaves. Butterflies fed on the nectar of flowers. Caterpillars seemed to destroy the conservatory's gardens as they consumed leaf after leaf, while butterflies were pollinating and beautifying them. How could caterpillars and butterflies that looked and behaved as differently as night and day, possibly come from the same egg?

A caterpillar's life begins as a larva that emerges from one of the eggs that a butterfly laid on the leaves of the same plant that will serve as food for their larva. These young caterpillars are congenitally programmed to be munching machines, and as they consume leaves, they often damage much of the same plant that offers them sustenance and shelter. They are self-centered, self-focused creatures, whose entire purpose in life is to satisfy their appetites. The world into which they have been hatched is limited to the leaves they see before them. Although caterpillars live in colonies, life is not about cooperating with their fellow caterpillars. It is all about individual survival and eating leaves, which as far as caterpillars know, will define their existence forever. They may have no idea that their intended genetic future is for them to become a new creature, a butterfly.

As caterpillars grow, they molt by sloughing off their tough exoskeletons. Being true to their nature, they eat that too. When they molt, some caterpillars may even change the color and pattern of their outer covering at certain stages of their lives. It is necessary for caterpillars to maintain their superficial protective covering so they can protect their hearts and their other organs. We can identify them by the image they present to the outside world, not by what is underneath the surface. When caterpillars have gone through several molts and are fully grown, they surround themselves in a chrysalis, otherwise known as a cocoon. As they hang helplessly in this cocoon, most of their organs and other structures dissolve and reform into organs, tissues, limbs and wings of the adults. After the adult butterflies emerge, they pump blood into their wings to expand them, and they spend the rest of their lives feeding on nectar and pollinating plants. Unfortunately, these beautiful butterflies only live for a few weeks to several months.

It appears that there was a lot of unnecessary energy expended in changing a caterpillar into a butterfly that is only going to live for such a short time. If caterpillars serve as food for small animals and birds, why expend the energy to make them into butterflies that also could be eaten by these animals? It is not as if butterflies are the only food source for a specific animal, nor are they the only creatures that could pollinate plants. Since there appears to be no obvious evolutionary advantage for this transformation, then changing from a caterpillar into a butterfly may have occurred for non-evolutionary reasons. This implies that butterflies may have been designed for a purpose by one with considerable imagination and intelligence.

With this possibility in mind, I begin my metaphor by explaining the analogy between the transformation of man's nature and the metamorphosis of a caterpillar into a butterfly. Most people believe that human beings have just one singular, unchangeable nature. Our universal acknowledgement and understanding of human nature is evident when we hear comments such as "Violence is just part of human nature," or "People behave like this all the time. It's just human nature." Throughout the remainder of the book, I will illustrate that human beings actually have two natures and will explain how one is transformed into the other.

Man is part of nature. He does not exist outside of it. So, it should be no surprise that God's process for transforming and rehabilitating man's selfish nature would resemble the metamorphosis of other animals in nature, such as tadpoles into frogs and, more specifically, caterpillars into butterflies. Since caterpillars are such primitive creatures, they could not possibly know anything about their Creator or His plans for their transformation. They seem only concerned with gorging themselves on leaves. They have no frame of reference for any other perspective on life other than their own. In order for caterpillars to grow, they have to molt their exoskeletons. This is a particularly dangerous time for these growing caterpillars because it leaves their vital organs more vulnerable to harsh weather and predators. It is as if they remove their protective covering so they can be open and accessible to their Creator's influence on their maturation.

The natural process of forming the chrysalis, in which a caterpillar undergoes its transformation into a butterfly, can only begin after he stops his gluttonous and destructive ways. In human terms, it is as if a person must repent and turn away from his self-centered way of living in order for God to initiate a dramatic change in him. Once he voluntarily encases his plump body in the protection of God's cocoon and his metamorphosis begins, all of his exoskeleton and most of his organs dissolve. It is as if he *dies unto himself* and places his future form and life in God's hands. While in his cocoon, God slowly remakes each larval caterpillar's body and transforms him into a delicate, beautiful butterfly, stripping away his old nature and giving him a new one. The caterpillar that emerges from his cocoon as a butterfly has essentially been born-again and literally sees the world with new eyes. He is now a new and wondrous example of God's handiwork, and he can use his newly developed wings to observe the world from God's elevated perspective.

God invested so much time and care into making His butterflies, yet their lives are extremely short, just as our lives are merely a blip on the timeline of eternity. Butterflies obeyed God's genetic command and submitted themselves into God's hands, and as a result, they have been freed from their primitive caterpillar bodies and their one dimensional lives. It is as if they have been blessed by their Creator and are capable of experiencing the same world in a brand new and exciting way. I doubt that there are any ungrateful butterflies.

If caterpillars had a choice to reject God's metamorphosis and did so, they would remain immature larvae for life. If they never repent, stop eating leaves and submit themselves into the hands of their Creator, they will never experience the abundant, enlightened life God had planned for them before they were born. These recalcitrant caterpillars will miss the opportunity to receive the nature of God and see life through His eyes. Unfortunately, in real life, some caterpillars do choose to remain caterpillars, while others choose to be transformed into butterflies. Therefore, the human race is comprised of both primitive caterpillars and the more advanced, intricately designed butterflies. I am going to extend this symbolism in my upcoming Biblical analogy of Genesis because this explanation will help you understand your true value and purpose and may change your life forever.

In the Bible, God said, "Let us make man in **our** image!" (Gen. 1:26) Then, He made His first two people, Adam and Eve, and gave them nearly free reign to roam in the Garden of Eden. Although God breathed life into His first two people, a defiant Eve and a disobedient Adam could not have possibly represented God's sterling image. These beings could not have been what God originally had in mind as the final form of His creation. Although God made them perfectly, His first two human creations did not possess His perfectly faithful and honest nature. However, since it was God who declared He would create man in His image, then God must be the one to complete the transformation of His rebellious humans into devoted, obedient and loving beings like Himself. As we know, regardless of the intelligence and capability caterpillar people may possess, they can not change their own nature. They may be able to control or improve their behavior at times, but they can never eliminate their self-serving, destructive, defiant caterpillar nature. A caterpillar can not use his own will and effort to change himself into a selfless and benevolent butterfly. He must place himself in the transforming vessel of God's cocoon, for only God can change him into a butterfly!

In order for God to transform mankind from caterpillars into butterflies, caterpillars must stop their consumption-focused, destructive behavior and surrender and humbly submit to God's authority before the Lord can finish their transformation. God will not trick them into submitting to Him, nor will He force them against their will. This would defeat God's plan and would be contrary to His nature. He wants us to surrender voluntarily to His authority and place our lives in His hands.

From the beginning of time, God had a plan to develop His selfless servant's heart and loving nature in Adam and Eve. Since God knew everything, including the future, it was no surprise to Him that the serpent, Satan would successfully tempt Adam and Eve into eating the forbidden fruit and they would be expelled from Eden. In fact, God was counting on it. There was something crucial missing in man's relationship with God that prevented God's human creation from assuming the full nature and likeness of their Creator, and that missing ingredient could only be obtained outside of the Garden of Eden.

What was yet to be established in God's relationship with man in the Garden of Eden was *love*. God thought His creation of Adam and Eve was good. They had a close relationship, but there was no mention of love from either party. Throughout the Bible, God commands us to love Him with all of our hearts, strength, and minds. Yet, this level of true love required a personal sacrifice, and neither Adam and Eve nor God had made any meaningful sacrifice for the other.

To establish the deepest love relationship possible, both God and His human creations would have to make the maximum sacrifice for each other. Jesus said in John 15:13 (NIV), "There is no greater love than to lay down one's life for one's friends." Since the Father, the Son, and the Holy Spirit represent the Holy Trinity, when the Father sent his only Son to die for our sins, God essentially sacrificed Himself to demonstrate His tremendous love for us. In order for us to show God our maximum love for Him, He expects us to reciprocate and voluntarily "die unto ourselves." But, what does "die unto ourselves" mean?

As progeny of Adam and Eve, we have a natural desire to be in control of our lives. If you do not believe me, just ask most teenagers waiting to attend college. They can not wait to be on their own and run their own lives. They do not want to be accountable to anyone, especially their parents, and certainly, not to God. All humans are born with this self-centered, caterpillar perspective on life and the deep psychological need for autonomy. Human beings have no genetic memory of what it was like to live in the Garden of Eden under God's authority. **Therefore, the caterpillar form of man naturally worships the Human Trinity: Me, Myself and I.**

What we love most is ourselves and our ability to be in control of our lives. Therefore, to "die unto ourselves," means giving up control of our lives. This makes sense because God is spirit. He does not want us to sacrifice our mortal lives to Him. He wants us to sacrifice our self-centered spirit to Him. So, in order to demonstrate our maximum love to God, we have to make the ultimate sacrifice to Him by killing off what we love more than anything else, our autonomy, like God did when He sacrificed what he loved most; His beloved Son, Jesus.

In practical terms, not only do we have to stop our self-serving gluttonous ways, we have to fire ourselves as the final director and authority of our lives. We must give control of our caterpillar lives back to God, not out of fear or obligation, but freely and voluntarily. Transferring our authority back to God allows us to restore the original, properly oriented relationship between man and God that Adam and Eve enjoyed in the Garden of Eden before their disobedience. As a result of our mutual sacrifice, we establish an unbreakable bond of love that will connect us together in a Holy relationship for eternity. God made us for His pleasure, but He also wanted us to have a loving relationship with Him, so we could share in His joy; His life. God knew we could not truly love Him until we surrendered control of our lives to Him.

Just as God created His original human caterpillars and believed they were very good, they were just the progenitors of God's final, adult form of His design, the butterfly stage of human metamorphosis. When these caterpillars submitted their lives to God, it certainly reunited them in a loving relationship with God, but it did not complete their transformation into His likeness, the image of Jesus. It was just the first step. God must do His transforming work on us in our cocoons to change us from little caterpillar gods into butterfly servants of God that reflect the giving nature of Jesus. Then, we will have the desire and capability of doing God's will rather than our own.

Jesus was sinless because He accomplished His Father's will perfectly. Doing God's will came naturally to Him, but recently born-again butterflies must learn to set aside their own self-importance, their own will, in order to begin doing God's will. In time, their relationship with God will grow stronger and more intimate. These new butterflies will make themselves more available for God to express His will and love through them. As butterflies mature under the watchful eyes of God and spiritually move nearer to Him, they will come to adopt God's worldview as their own and more closely resemble the image of God. Unfortunately, they will never become totally mature and look exactly like Jesus. Even beautiful butterflies can only represent the image of God, not become God. When you think about it, it is safer to remain merely in the image of God. It was Adam and Eve's desire to be like God that got the rest of us caterpillars in trouble in the first place.

Now that butterflies have a loving, trusting relationship with their Creator, He can finish making His butterflies into people that love their neighbors as themselves rather than caterpillar people who love to be served by them. **The true purpose of a human being is to love and serve God and his neighbors.** A caterpillar person can serve others, as well, but he tends to do it for selfish reasons with the ultimate goal of glorifying himself, not God. Therefore, regardless how many meritorious deeds a caterpillar does during his lifetime or how exceptional a person he may have been, a caterpillar can never represent the image of God. Niceness is a personality trait given to caterpillars by God, and if they were fortunate, their parents cultivated their kind demeanor and encouraged their helpful behavior.

Butterflies may become nicer people through their transformation.

However, niceness in itself is not the true measure of success of our Christian transformation. Therefore, the goal of human life is not to become an exceptionally civil caterpillar. It is to become a new person that possesses the grace and character of Jesus. God wants us to become butterflies with wings that will allow us to see the world from His perspective and ascend to Heaven when our mortal lives end. Only caterpillars that have surrendered their lives to the true God, through the acceptance of Christ's sacrifice for them on the cross, can become butterflies. **Man can never be transformed by merely proclaiming his belief in God. He must surrender his will and authority to God, and in so doing, relinquish ownership and control of his life to Him.**

How do we know if we have truly surrendered to God's authority? How do we know if we have truly become butterflies? Certainly our anatomy remains unchanged. So, what has changed inside of us? We will know in our hearts that we have surrendered to God when the world in which we live seems different and new, as if we were seeing it for the very first time. We will be less focused on ourselves and more on our spouses, families and friends. Life will become more about pleasing God and seeking to do His will, rather than praying for Him to serve ours. Once we are transformed into butterflies, we will truly believe that God owns the world and everything in it. We will be able to accept the fact that He owns us; our bodies, our minds, our possessions, our wealth, our children and our spouses. God is our Creator. He made our world, and He is the master of it. We are not. We will find ourselves more frequently giving credit to God and thanking Him for our blessings. Once we have surrendered to God, He can finish making us in His likeness, and as God's new creation, we can become a visible testimony and reflection of His personality and character.

Those of us, who have been transformed into butterflies, believe that our unique personalities, gifts, talents and intellect came from God rather than the roll of the genetic dice. **Surrendered people accept being a slave to God, for we remember how horrible it was being**

a slave to our self-centered nature. Our former lives had been a quest for power, possessions, pleasure and position because that was the measure of our personal significance and worldly success. Yet, as butterflies, it is remarkable how much less significant material wealth becomes. When our worldview changes, we realize how quickly we can be separated from our money. As a consequence of our surrender to God's authority, we stop believing that money is our source of security, and we start to pursue a closer relationship with the God of the Universe. He promises that we can never be separated from His love and have our joy taken from us. As butterflies, we are able to see the world from God's perspective and, for the first time, life and death makes perfect sense.

There is one obstacle for butterflies when it comes to permanently surrendering to God. We are able to use our wings to lift us onto God's altar, where we bow our heads in gratitude and prayer at the foot of Christ's cross. However, we can not nail ourselves to it forever. Our new butterfly wings insure our salvation, but we still have legs, which we occasionally use to walk away from the lordship of Christ. We tend to crawl off the altar when we become impatient waiting for God to answer our prayers or intervene in our lives. Surrendering our will to Jesus has to be done many times per day. We should not feel guilty about our repeated retreat from the cross. Remember, guilt is from Satan and conviction is from God. Guilt paralyzes us. Conviction motivates us to change. Once we are convicted of our misbehavior, we should fly right back. God knows that submission is a process, a way of life, not the last step in the recipe for sanctification. The benefit of being a butterfly rather than a caterpillar is that we will feel God's peace with every return to the cross. If the caterpillar happens to encounter the cross, he will feel nothing. To him, it is just another piece of wood.

Therefore, a caterpillar that refuses to surrender his life to God can have no real hope for an eternal future with God. Jesus proclaimed, "For whoever would save his life will lose it, but whoever loses his life for my sake and the gospel's will save it" (Mark 8:35 ESV).

If a caterpillar ignores or rejects Jesus, He rejects God's gracious gift to become a butterfly. Although men may have started life as caterpillars, they were ultimately designed to become butterflies that can wing their way through life and return home to Heaven when their short lives come to an end.

Since Heaven is God's home and God is perfect, His home must be a pure, peaceful, and perfect place. If His home is to stay that way, God cannot admit little, self-centered, caterpillar gods that can not wait to walk over others in an attempt to eat everyone's manna. If this were the case, God's home would just be a replica of our current selfish, dysfunctional and chaotic world on Earth. In order for Heaven to remain pure and perfect, we caterpillars must place our faith in Jesus and trust Him to become the boss, the CEO, the president, the king, and the master of our lives. Once we establish Christ as our new master, our sins will be forgiven, and we can be made into newborn butterflies acceptable before God. Limiting Heaven's inhabitants to God-centered butterflies ensures that Heaven will be free of conflict and remain a peaceful and joyful place. Can you imagine billions of butterflies folding their wings in unity and prayer before their Creator? What a breathtaking picture of beauty and serenity that would be! Heaven was made for butterflies. And, only God can make a butterfly!

The Nature of Caterpillar and Butterfly Men

Our world is inhabited by two types of fully operational human beings, each possessing remarkably different natures. Although each possesses equal intellect and abilities, they see the world from opposite perspectives. These opposing worldviews result in the divergent way they perceive the world and live their lives. Caterpillars can see only what they saw when they were born — leaves for their consumption. All caterpillars' lives are about gorging themselves on leaves. They can not imagine that there is anything more to life than experiencing the pleasure of filling their bellies and trying to survive in a dangerous world. Both caterpillar and butterfly brains are functioning properly, but their contrasting view of the same world leads each to different conclusions, which result in different and sometimes conflicting goals and behavior. A man's perspective on life determines his worldview, and it is man's worldview that ultimately determines his interpretation and understanding of reality. **Unfortunately, two different conclusions regarding the same reality can not both be true.**

Caterpillar men are born with a self-preservation instinct, which serves as the foundation for their self-centered perspective and self-serving behavior. The way they live their lives is similar to a real caterpillar's way of life, which is to consume all the leaves they can until they are full, which never seems to happen. Caterpillars live to fulfill their primal urges and desires. Their self-centered nature allows them to be indifferent to whose gardens they consume and damage in the process. They want what they want, and they want it now. They have little concern over whom they have to crawl to get it.

The caterpillar man's philosophy of life is: Ask not what you can do for others, but what others can do for you. Their view of life depends on what the world can provide them. Since their appetites are voracious, and they live as if there is no greater power and authority other than themselves, they must call upon their own wits to locate and secure all the leaves they can consume. Caterpillars also believe they are to live outside the authority of God, so they can remain free from His moral code regarding their behavior. They worship the power of their natural-born intellect, which they mistakenly see as considerable. This self-worship prevents them from submitting to any higher authority that might give them a new life and worldview. Sadly, caterpillars condemn themselves to remain prisoners in the bodies of lowly larvae. How smart can even the most well-educated caterpillars be, who condemn themselves to a life of never-ending work, feeding on their own and everyone else's gardens because they refuse to submit themselves to a higher authority?

The butterfly person, on the other hand, submits his body and his will to God, as if his former caterpillar self has been set aside to make room for his butterfly nature. As his new nature develops, it overtakes his old caterpillar nature and his urges and compulsion to consume no longer dominate him. These former caterpillars have repented and committed themselves to lie still before God, and trust Him to remake them while they hang helplessly in their cocoons. This is consistent with what the Apostle Paul said in II Corinthians 5:17 (NLT), "This means that anyone who belongs to Christ has become a new person. The old life is gone; the new life has begun!" These caterpillar people chose to place their faith *in Christ*, which correlates to real caterpillars enclosing themselves in their cocoons (God's hands). While they hung helplessly under God's authority and control, He sustained them during their transformation. They waited patiently for God to make them into His new creation. God not only gave them a new nature, He gave them His nature. When His new creations emerged from God's life-changing cocoon as butterflies, they were able to experience life from God's higher and more virtuous perspective.

These new butterflies are now able to see their former caterpillar thought processes and behavior as immature and dysfunctional. For the first time, they can recognize and admit to the evil that was ingrained in their self-centered nature. They could not see it before. **The butterfly man's philosophy has changed and is now: Ask not what others can do for you, but what you can do for others.** Unlike caterpillars that consume people's gardens, butterflies now see the world from God's perspective and accept that everything is a gift from God that is to be shared and used for the benefit of themselves and others. They still feed on flowering plants, but instead of gluttonously consuming them to the brink of destruction, they have been redesigned to pollinate people's gardens. In fact, as they float from flower to flower, adding beauty and interest to the garden, they produce more food through pollination for themselves and their caterpillar neighbors. In human terms, butterflies are supposed to serve, produce and provide for others in need. Unlike caterpillars, their new worldview and corresponding nature dictates that they use things and love people, not vice versa. Their nature has changed from that of their fellow caterpillar by virtue of their choice to give up living as their own god, and begin living under the authority of their original Creator, who is their true God.

The human caterpillar's perspective on life can truly be transformed by merely changing the authority under which he lives! This change in perspective determines his worldview, which represents a new understanding of his life and the reality of the world around him. God knew that if he wanted to give a caterpillar a new nature, His nature, He would first have to give him a new perspective. To accomplish this, He had to finish making His original, primal caterpillar into His likeness, by transforming him into a butterfly. No matter how benevolent or spiritual a caterpillar becomes, he can never see the world from a butterfly's perspective. He will never be able to assume the nature of a butterfly and possess the loving nature of Christ.

We must remember that, although caterpillars remain in the incomplete, immature form of a human being without God's transformation, God equally loves and values His caterpillars and butterflies. Remember, caterpillars needed to exist first, for without them, there could be no butterflies. In fact, God so loved His caterpillar creation, He sacrificed His life for all of His little, lost larvae, while they were still sinners pretending to be their own god. It makes no difference to God whether his caterpillars are Christian, Catholic, Muslim, Jewish, Hindu, Buddhist or Atheists. (Yes, atheism is a religion. Their god and worshipper are one and the same.) Jesus came to rescue all of His caterpillar people from their religions, so He could transform them into authentic butterfly men and women. We have no reason to look down upon the unsaved caterpillar because we butterflies were these same caterpillars just one decision ago. In fact, God commands us to love them as ourselves, and Christ commissions us to spread the Gospel throughout the world to these stiff-necked, clueless caterpillars. God was not willing to have even one of His lost larvae remain separated from Him.

Chapter Three
Dynamics of Dysfunction: Primacy and Significance

For where you have envy and selfish ambition, there you find disorder and every evil practice.

James 3:16 NIV

"Whatever makes men good Christians, makes them good citizens."

Daniel Webster

Dysfunctional living occurs as a result of having the wrong worldview. The more dysfunctional we behave the more harm we do to ourselves, our relationships and other people. The worldview that results in healthier, more fulfilling relationships and assists us in countering our evil natures represents the correct worldview.

I have asserted that adhering to the wrong worldview leads to dysfunctional living. What does it mean to be "dysfunctional?" It simply means to not fully or optimally function. As a result of being dysfunctional, we do not interact with others in ways that lead to healthy and harmonious relationships. Medically speaking, leading a dysfunctional life is like having a blockage in one or two of our coronary arteries. We have enough blood flow to keep us alive, but circulation is so substantially diminished, the heart barely provides the body enough power to walk a block. As a result of this impairment, we are unable to function to our full capacity.

In Biblical terms, when we live in a manner that falls outside of the will and design of God, or falls short of the glory of God, we call it *sin*. In the Greek language, sin means "missing the mark." In medical terms, "missing the mark" means dysfunction. I know it is common to think of sin as "bad" because bad things happen to us and others when we sin. However, sin is actually a consequence of not operating under God's control, and because of this, we do not behave according to God's design and purpose. For example, assume we are a perfectly designed TV with the picture and volume controls in working order. If the TV's volume and channel selectors begin to change on their own rather than under the control of the person operating the remote, we would consider the TV to be malfunctioning. If the TV had been **willfully** changing the settings, we would consider its behavior to be **sinful**. For the TV to be functioning properly, it would have to be appropriately responding to the one person operating the remote, for he is in control. The TV represents man, and God is the one who should be in control of the remote.

Since caterpillars live and operate outside of God's control, they are considered dysfunctional. They did not choose to be dysfunctional. They were born this way. They are dysfunctional because they see themselves as the central figure in their lives, which I believe starts at birth for all of us. My logic regarding the biological primacy of human beings goes like this: As infants, we are totally dependent upon our parents to feed, clothe and care for us. Yet, as a consequence of our parent's continual attention, we begin to see ourselves at the center of our world. Unfortunately, we conclude that the goal of our lives is to be served by others. Thus, we are born with a self-centered perspective.

Ironically, our self-centered nature does not develop from being self-reliant. It is a result of our natural dependence upon the efforts of others to serve and support us. The newborn's determination that he is the primary person in his life was an incorrect assessment and, therefore, he adopted a perspective regarding his future that was based on a lie. In the Bible, man's belief that he could be like God was suggested to them by the serpent Satan, the Father of Lies. Both Adam and Eve and their caterpillar progeny began their new lives believing a lie. This lie resulted in their separation from God, which condemned them to dysfunctional living and unnecessary hardship. The Bible describes the dysfunctional nature of man as being "born in sin" which you can see begins immediately after our birth. Because of our self-centered perspective, we are born with the inclination to live under our own authority, which means we are born with a sinful nature.

Without the knowledge or acceptance of a God greater than ourselves, we see ourselves as the primary person in our lives. This is called *primacy*. The need for primacy is a product of our self-preservation instinct, so it is as much a biological function as a psychological one. Our need for primacy can be suppressed for short periods of time i.e. individual acts of self-denial and selfless, heroic acts of courage, but this behavior occurs infrequently. **The lower our sense of significance and specialness, the greater is our need to see ourselves as the primary person in our lives. The greater our need for primacy, which is the emotional and psychological belief that our needs must be satisfied first, the more likely we are to neglect, delay, or deny fulfilling the needs of others.** Our need for primacy also drives us to impose our will on other people, whose importance, by definition, must be *secondary* to our own. In order to reinforce our sense of primacy, we will wield power over others to elevate our relative sense of importance and value in society. The greater our need to impose our will, the more harm we are capable of doing to others. Those, who do the greatest harm to others, are considered *evil*. Therefore, since all people feel less significant at times, everyone has the potential for evil behavior, for it is part of man's nature as self-centered beings. **Man's sense of primacy and his need for significance are the psychological foundations for his evil nature.**

Although many caterpillar people may not believe in God, they still have a universal understanding that God is the master; the primary, supreme, being, who controls everything. Since caterpillars have not yet submitted their lives to God, psychologically, they still see themselves as the primary person in their lives and believe they are in total control of their destiny. In order for caterpillars to live as their own master, just as God is His own master, they think their lives are centered on serving their will and fulfilling their desires. In order for them to maintain their role as their own god, they must reassure themselves of their superior intellect and primary importance in their lives. They must appear more powerful and intelligent. Therefore, they expect their opinions to be accepted as the final word. Since they function as their own god, their assessments, their decisions, and their will must prevail or their god-like self image might be threatened or proven false. Most of the time, these thoughts are subliminal, so they are not necessarily aware of them. These pretend caterpillar gods will use, abuse, or manipulate anyone, even their own family in order to fulfill their will. Life becomes a mind game, and the goal is to maintain the lie that they, like God, are in control of their lives and the lives of others.

The caterpillars' god-like sense of primacy causes them to believe that they should have authority over caterpillars and butterflies alike, just as we butterflies understand that God has authority and control over all of us. Therefore, caterpillars have a natural belief that their needs are more important than their neighbor's. This assumption of primacy makes their relationships with others unequally balanced. **Because they live under their own authority, they subconsciously see themselves as the god of their lives, which justifies their manipulation or oppression of others to make themselves feel more significant.** Caterpillar people do not possess the perspective that gives them the humility to accept the fact that there may be many people and circumstances in life that are beyond their control. Subconsciously, they know that they can not control everyone. Yet, they have their god-like image to protect, so they must prevent having their weaknesses or failings exposed. In order to accomplish this, they will utilize their intellect and the power of their personalities to try to control other people's opinion of them and situations in which they find themselves. **In order to justify their position of god-like primacy and authority, caterpillars must see themselves as being in control.**

Caterpillar people are also compelled to reassure themselves of their significance. Subconsciously, they must continually reinforce their sense of value and specialness by sustaining their god-like opinion of themselves. They are unaware that a supreme being made them, so they can not fathom that their Creator had already conferred upon them a specific value or a designated purpose. As far as caterpillars know, they must earn their own value and significance. Even a lowly caterpillar knows it would be absurd to declare himself special in the eyes of other people. This notion that an individual's value is determined by other people is reflected in such common sayings as, "beauty is in the eye of the beholder" and "property is only worth what someone is willing to pay for it." **Although caterpillar people place themselves at the center of their lives, they can only see themselves as valuable if others appear to value them.**

It should be no surprise that we humans frequently do not function properly since we are born into this world with no instruction manual. Our self-preservation instinct may tell us how to survive, but we have no specific directions regarding the manner in which we are to relate to others and live our lives. We are totally dependent upon our parents and other adults to teach us proper relational skills. Unfortunately, it is merely a matter of chance that we will be the children of responsible, moral, and wise parents. At birth, we have no knowledge of God's existence, and without directly knowing Him, we could never know our true value and purpose. Today, everything from cowbells to computers comes with instructions, but we humans, the most complex entity of all, emerge from our package without even a note. God was either playing a trick on his creatures, or as the manufacturer, He prepared our instruction manual (the Bible) well in advance, and there was just no room in the womb to include such a book. When you think about it, if we came with instructions, only the girls would read them. The boys would probably meander aimlessly through life rather than ask for directions. Since both men and women have equal access to the Bible, neither gender must remain dysfunctional caterpillars for their entire lives. However, in our self-centered state, just reading the Bible's instructions for living, without surrendering our authority to God, does not guarantee us the ability to understand and obey them.

The only way for a caterpillar person to gain a new nature is to surrender the authority and control of his life to God and be born again as a butterfly. Since a butterfly person has been transformed by God, he accepts living under God's control, and while living under His control makes him more functional, it does not make him perfect. **If a butterfly man could perfectly live under God's authority and always did His will, He would be called Jesus.** Human beings can not perfectly do God's will. In fact, since we are born self-centered, not God-centered, we break the First Commandment, "You must not have any other god but me" (Exodus 20:3 NLT) as soon as we take our first breath. If there can be a little dysfunction in even the most mature butterfly's life, imagine the amount of dysfunction in an immature caterpillar's life. Our parents can teach us to be less dysfunctional, but if they do not introduce us to Christ and the Biblical worldview, we can never become truly functional.

I have spent more than half of my adult life as a caterpillar, and I was dysfunctional that entire time. As a young man, I was an outstanding athlete and honors scholar. I succeeded in anything I tried and was just as gifted when it came to dysfunctional living. Perhaps my religious roots contributed to my confusion and dysfunction. My mother was Jewish, and my father was Catholic. Occasionally, Passover fell on Easter. Having to fast on Passover kept me from eating my Italian grandmother's homemade spaghetti and meatballs on Easter. No child should ever have to experience such a sacrifice. I'm fortunate to have survived.

I did not learn much religion from my Jewish and Catholic parents, except that guilt and fear, respectively, were part of each. For the next three decades, I lived as a functional atheist. I was the caterpillar's caterpillar. I was a hard worker and over-achiever. I thought all I needed to do to be successful was to use the power of my education, intellect and personality. I studied hard and graduated near the top of my high school and college classes and went through medical school in just over three years instead of four. In contrast, I was shy, lacked confidence in myself with girls and my sense of self-worth was totally based on my performance and achievements. I rarely drank, never had a cup of coffee or smoked a single cigarette. I never tried a single illicit or prescription drug and never had a brush with the law. As a caterpillar, I dutifully *crawled* the straight and narrow.

I had a nearly perfect behavior record, yet when I was 36, my marriage of nine years ended in a nasty divorce and a broken home and family. I was so depressed I could barely function at all. After the divorce, the more I insisted that my ex-wife treat me with the level of appreciation and respect I desired, the more recalcitrant she became. I can remember her saying that I was trying to manipulate her, and many years after the fact, I recognized that she was correct. Her outright rejection of me hurt terribly. Living without my children made me fear the future as a parent. I felt compelled to try to prevent her from causing me additional unbearable pain. The more I tried to protect myself from her, the more she thought I was manipulating her. After the divorce, my relationship with my ex-wife became so strained that I went without seeing my children for nearly four years. I missed them terribly, but because of my self-centeredness and my pride, coupled with her stubbornness or fear of future confrontations, my reconnection with them did not occur until my daughter was sixteen and could drive. After seven long years of emotional distress and the emptiness of not being a father to my children, the arrival of my newborn daughter helped me recover the sense of family and parenthood that I lost in the divorce.

My unhelpful caterpillar attempts to take control in order to improve an awful situation resulted from my self-centered worldview. My sense of primacy kicked in, so attending to my hurt feelings was psychologically imperative. This was not even a conscious event. As a caterpillar, it came natural for me to put my needs before others, and occasionally they came before my children's needs, as well. Psychologically, I viewed the divorce from the perspective of how it affected me first and others second. Instead of using my intellectual abilities and reason to begin rebuilding my strained relationships with my children, I followed my emotional need to rebuild my male ego and restore my sense of self-righteousness. It was my sense of primacy and my need to re-establish my own significance that drove me to behave as I did. In trying to live according to Satan's lie, which was that I had the power to control events and people in my life, I directed my marriage and divorce by myself rather than depending on God to guide and restrain me.

Since I lived life as my own god, I believed there was no superior being to call upon to quell my fear and reassure myself that I still had a future. Therefore, I became my own worst enemy. I was so broken and so negative, the only life I could see ahead of me was one filled with endless emotional pain, loneliness and permanent separation from my children. Without the true God in my life, I believed it was up to me to remedy my horrible situation. However, deep inside, I knew I was not capable of controlling my ex-wife or anything else in my life at that time. I was more than brokenhearted. I was a broken man. I should have known that since I was not able to control my wife's behavior during my marriage, it was foolish to expect to do so during and after the divorce. The more I tried to protect my self-image and my parental position, the angrier I became. The divorce separated me from my children, and I was forced into court to secure my rights to see my kids. I was so upset and angry during the court proceedings, the children I was fighting to see, were hesitant to be around me. Sadly, my self-centered nature made it impossible to put my pain aside and focus on the pain and grief my children were experiencing. The harder I tried to gain control of the situation and put a stop to my pain, the more pain I experienced. I had functioned as my own god my entire life and my life had become entirely dysfunctional. Because I lived life under my own control, my life went out of control. My god failed me! And, I had no one to blame but myself.

Imagine how much more peaceful life would have been for me and my family, if I had fired myself as the lord of my life and made Jesus my Lord and Savior. I could have asked Him to intervene for me rather than trying to repair the rift in my marriage by myself. I could have been a butterfly who folded his wings in prayer, instead of using my many caterpillar legs to climb over and around a tragic situation. I should have known better. I had no training to function as my own god. If I could have given control of myself, my ex-wife and my children's lives to Jesus, I would have avoided trying to take control of my separation and divorce in order to lessen or eliminate my pain. If I had put my faith in God, rather than calling upon my wits to try to control my ex-wife's behavior, I could have called upon Him and used His power to help me endure my pain and frustration. Jesus could have given me His peace in those stormy times, and I might have become less angry and more appealing to my young children. If I had not behaved as my own god, I would have abandoned trying to change my ex-wife and avoided a lot of unnecessary anger and frustration. Instead, I could have called upon God to guide and change me. I was like Adam. I thought that all it took to be god was to be my own boss and call the shots, yet my life before and during my divorce was filled with anxiety, frustration, worry, pain and bouts of depression. I learned that when human beings live without God at the center of their lives, they become dysfunctional (sinful). Sin is more than just breaking one of the Ten Commandments. Anything we do; good or bad that is performed outside of the authority and will of Christ is sinful. **If we do not accept that God is God, and we are not, we will inevitably live dysfunctional and unnecessarily painful and unhappy lives.**

As I look back, I became an expert in the process of separation and divorce, because I made every mistake a man can make while going through this gut-wrenching experience. I certainly learned many valuable truths about life, but I do not recommend this form of education to anyone. Years later, after I became a follower of Jesus, God took what I learned about divorce in the school of hard knocks, and led me to get involved in my church's divorce recovery ministry, which I have led for nearly a decade. To paraphrase the Bible, God can turn what man meant for evil, to the good of those who love Him, and are called according to His purpose. (Romans 8:28) He used my pain and long-suffering to help alleviate the pain of others going through their ego-crushing and life-changing divorces. The Lord works in mysterious ways, yet always according to His logical and purposeful plan for those who surrender to His authority.

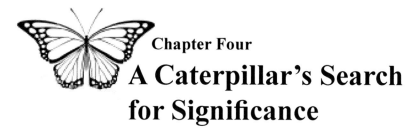

Chapter Four

A Caterpillar's Search for Significance

This is how God showed his love among us: He sent his one and only Son into the world that we might live through him. This is love: not that we loved God, but that he loved us and sent his Son as an atoning sacrifice for our sins.

1 John 4:9-10 NIV

"Oh, eternal and everlasting God, direct my thoughts, words and work. Wash away my sins in the immaculate blood of the Lamb and purge my heart by thy Holy Spirit. Daily, frame me more and more in the likeness of thy son, Jesus Christ, that living in thy fear, and dying in thy favor, I may in thy appointed time obtain the resurrection of the justified unto eternal life. Bless, O Lord, the whole race of mankind and let the world be filled with the knowledge of thee and thy son, Jesus Christ."

George Washington

No human being expects to live his entire life without leaving a memorable impression on those with whom he shared his life. If, at any time during his life, he believes that he is insignificant to others, he will lose the purpose and will to live. Therefore, establishing an adequate level of significance is extremely vital to caterpillars and butterflies. The question is: Who will determine our significance, human beings or God?

Caterpillars Get Their Significance from Man

Caterpillar people seek to gain their sense of significance by trying to earn the good opinion and approval of others. Unfortunately, being good to others does not come easily to caterpillar people because the natural man is not born with a genetic predisposition to treat others better than himself. In fact, when he is stressed, his self-preservation instinct compels him to care less for others and more for himself, which occasionally causes him to be cruel or heartless to his fellow man. A self-centered, caterpillar man can choose to perform meritorious deeds, but subconsciously, he does so to satisfy his own emotional and psychological needs. The beneficial effect he may have on his neighbor is usually secondary. His good deeds tend to resemble a trade or manipulation, not love.

Jesus reinforced this idea that the caterpillar man is not good, in Mark 10:18 (NIV), when He said "No one is good-except God alone." Only God has a good nature. Man has an evil one. The self-centered man is not naturally good to others because, as his own god, his psychological perspective dictates that others are less important than himself. Even, Almighty God takes second place or may have no place at all in his life. Since submission to God is the absolute prerequisite for being obedient to God, and it is obedience that leads to selfless deeds, then caterpillars are not generally good. For genuine goodness to come from man, God's goodness must flow through him. Therefore, only butterflies can be truly selfless in the performance of their good deeds.

Caterpillars tend to be the primary psychological beneficiaries of their own good deeds. They are motivated to perform good deeds because their deeds make them feel good about themselves, or they help them appear good to others. For example, Hitler performed enough good deeds to keep Eva Braun as his mistress for over fifteen years, yet no one would consider him to be the paragon of goodness. **The truth is that man's ability to perform good deeds does not mean he is basically good.**

A caterpillar's value tends to come more from the image he presents to others, and less from the actual effect his good deeds have on others. Therefore, the caterpillar person tends to boast about his compassionate intentions, thus receiving a nearly immediate positive response and emotional reward. Because he receives his emotional reward before he performs his benevolent deed, he can receive the psychological benefit without a single positive achievement. In time, proclaiming his intentions become so emotionally rewarding that his focus on fulfilling his promise to do good deeds becomes less and less important.

In the first half of Psalm 14:1 (NIV), it says that only fools say in their hearts, "There is no God." Any caterpillar man who denies the existence and authority of God, by default, lives as his own god. And, any man who denies God's existence makes it impossible for him to realize that he is loved, valued and significant to God. Consequently, he has no other option but to obtain his significance from human beings. **Just like a man who represents himself in a court of law has a fool for an attorney, a man who tries to live his life under his own authority has a fool for a god.** Therefore, in his attempt to be his own master, he condemns himself to be a slave to the opinion and approval of his neighbor.

Because caterpillars were foolish enough to deny the existence or belief in God, they have placed themselves in this dependent predicament. The caterpillar man thinks he is living his own life, but he is actually living the life others expect of him. In an effort to please others, he will work himself to the bone to acquire enough possessions and wealth to impress his neighbors. Others may work tirelessly to train themselves to become accomplished musicians, athletes, or performers so that others will admire or respect them. Many will diet and exercise to the point of pain or exhaustion, and spend a fortune on clothes in order to present an image to others that will make themselves feel desired. Caterpillars need to develop their image, so they can achieve positions of power and influence so that other people revere and serve them. They must find a way to be seen in a positive light. Caterpillars are psychologically driven to go to enormous lengths to present an image of success to others so that they will feel relevant and appear significant in our world.

For caterpillars, image is everything! Their worth is totally defined and dependent upon how they are viewed by others. Like real caterpillars in nature, they allow others to see only what is on the surface. Their hearts are enclosed in their tough exoskeleton and are hidden from most people. Since their significance is a product of their outward appearance, the condition of their hearts and the content of their character matters less to caterpillars. **Therefore, it is more beneficial and takes less effort for the caterpillar to** *appear* **significant to others rather than truly** *become* **significant to others.**

It is ironic to me that caterpillars spend so much of their time trying to earn the approval of the same people, whose needs they believe are less important and for whom they care very little. It's been said that many people "spend money they don't have on things they don't need to impress people they don't like." How true! If they realized how little time others spent thinking about them, they would not spend so much time worrying about what others thought about them. They forget that the other caterpillars are naturally as self-centered as they are and seldom think about anyone else but themselves.

Although the caterpillar's desire for significance and superiority is the driving force that causes him to achieve extraordinary things, it is also this same need for significance that compels him to put his fellow man down in order to elevate his own sense of importance. If he can not legitimately earn his significance, he might demean, belittle or abuse others in order to raise his own relative level of personal importance. The lower a caterpillar's sense of self-importance, the more force or power he will be willing to use against another person in order to correct this perceived power imbalance. He may even resort to violence or murder in order to prove to himself and others that he is more powerful and distinctive enough to remain the central character in his life.

A case in point is the Virginia Tech shootings in 2007, when Seung-Hui Cho, an emotionally disturbed student went on a shooting spree on campus. I recall in one of the news reports that he signed some of his schoolwork with a *question mark*. Here was a young man who was unsure of his value and identity as a person, and falsely concluded that it was other students that were oppressing and devaluing him. In order to quell his anxiety and re-establish his sense of significance, he needed to regain control over his perceived persecutors. Tragically, he chose to use massive force to make his point. He armed himself to the teeth and callously murdered 32 innocent people before turning his gun on himself. It is tragic that his targets had to be wounded or killed before he realized that murdering his imagined oppressors had not restored his sense of significance. After the killings, he felt remorse because he finally understood that this planned execution was not the remedy to his low sense of personal value, and he committed suicide. This is exactly how Judas Iscariot reacted after he betrayed Christ. He thought thirty pieces of silver were more valuable to him than continuing his relationship with Jesus, the Son of God. When he finally realized that he had been the victim of Satan's standard lie, which is to love things and use people, he felt so remorseful he hung himself from a bridge.

Man does not have to malfunction to exhibit harmful or destructive behavior. Evil is ingrained in his nature. It is the caterpillar man's emotional need for significance and control, coupled with his god-like belief that his emotional or physical needs should be satisfied first, that is the psychological foundation for the existence of evil in the mind of man. **It is man's self-centeredness that is the source of all evil in our world!**

Self-Centeredness and Pride

If it is man's self-centered nature that is the foundation of all evil in the world, then how does pride fit into the equation? Proverbs 16:18 (NIV) says, "Pride goes before destruction, a haughty spirit before a fall." It was the spirit of pride that made Adam and Eve think they could compete with the greatness of God by merely obtaining more knowledge. It was pride that prompted them to disobey God's one and only rule not to eat from the tree of knowledge, and this disobedience led to their fall from grace.

Satan also fell from God's grace by believing that he could possibly surpass God's greatness. As C.S. Lewis wrote in *Mere Christianity*, "it was through pride that the devil became the devil." I know of no better description of pride and its effect on human beings than that found in *Mere Christianity*. In the next several paragraphs, I will include several of Lewis' thoughts and insights to help us gain a greater understanding of pride. So, let's begin.

Another word for self-centeredness is non-God-centeredness. Lewis seemed to understand this when he said, "Pride is the complete anti-God state of mind." Only a non-God-centered person would even dare to compare his status and authority to God's. If a person's worldview does not make a man think he is absolutely nothing compared to God, he will start comparing himself to Him, perhaps, not in power, but in importance. As a man grows in knowledge, he begins to believe that he can compete with God for control of his life. Man's pride causes him to believe he can ultimately replace God as his master. Therefore, as Lewis proclaims, "pride does more than make us competitive. Pride is, by its nature, competitive."

In his chapter, *The Great Sin,* Lewis describes pride as not merely desiring material wealth and power; it is the compulsion to have more than the next man. The spirit of pride forces the prideful person to be in constant competition with others in order to see who will be the top dog. The sole effect of pride is to create a superior image. Therefore, merely possessing things are never enough. Since he must have more than the next man, he will never be able to find pleasure in his current possessions or his level of power. The prideful person needs to have more than his neighbor because his significance is determined in this manner. Just being rich is not enough to satisfy him. He must be richer than the other man because he needs others to admire him. Lewis concludes that the prideful man will never be content with his "own admiration." In this state of mind, he can never love his neighbor or anyone else because they are, by definition, his lifelong competitors. Lewis says, "Pride is spiritual cancer: it eats up the very possibility of love, or contentment, or even common sense." Lewis goes on to say that "greed and selfishness are the result of pride, but it is power that he really enjoys. If he perceives one as more powerful, that person becomes his rival and enemy…. Pride always means enmity; it is enmity. And not only enmity between man and man, but enmity to God."

The evil nature of the self-centered, prideful man rears its ugly head through competition. I am not referring to any athletic or ordinary competitions, but competitions for individual value and significance. Pride is also exhibited on both ends of the personality spectrum. It can affect the inadequate personality type or the narcissist. The inadequate person's sense of pride compels him to compete for the affirmation of people, who have a low opinion of him. If he can not earn and raise his significance in the eyes of others, he may slander them to elevate his own sense of significance or slay them to display his power over them. **It is his self-centered nature that allows pride to incite him to perpetrate evil upon his neighbor.**

The same is true of the narcissist, who seems to have everything; power, possessions and position. Since he does not have a God-centered perspective on life, his pride will cause him to find others utterly insignificant, and he will become oblivious to their feelings or needs. This type of prideful person, who cares nothing about others, can perpetrate the greatest evil because he sees them as worthless pawns to be used or sacrificed for his own desires. Whether a man has an inferiority or superiority complex, without having a God-centered nature, his pride will inevitably make him the source of harm and evil towards his fellow man.

The spirit of pride permeates our world like the air we breathe, but fortunately, there is a straightforward way to reduce its influence and ultimately render it harmless to ourselves and our neighbors.

The basis of pride is competition for significance. Therefore, eliminating the need to compete for significance renders the devil's spirit of pride impotent. The only way to eliminate the need for a person to compete for his own significance is to have Jesus freely bestow it upon him, so he no longer must earn it from his fellow man. This gift is only available to a caterpillar that is willing to be transformed into a God-centered butterfly.

Butterflies Get Their Significance from Jesus

Since caterpillars have no innate understanding that God made them, they can only assume that they came into existence by chance. People who believe their lives are a result of the roll of the evolutionary dice are, by definition, no more remarkable or valuable than anything or anyone else. The Great Deceiver, Satan, wanted us to believe in evolutionary theory. It was the perfect vehicle to keep man separated from God. As long as man did not come to know God, he would continue to believe he had no intrinsic worth. Without intrinsic worth, he would have to earn his significance from his neighbors, which makes him a slave to their opinion. Let me clarify what I mean by the word *slaves*. Simply stated, slaves are people, who live totally under the authority of the person in control.

After Satan had deceived Adam and Eve into disobeying God, they were banished from Eden. **Satan did not have to force Adam and Eve to worship him. He merely needed to encourage them and their descendants to worship themselves, so we would remain disconnected from God.** Unfortunately, total and unconditional submission of one's life to *oneself* is also slavery. Therefore, when we attempt to live as our own god, we become slaves to our self-centered nature and, subsequently, to the approval of our neighbors. Without God involved our lives, we are easily deceived into believing that self-focus and self-indulgence is the only way to live an independent life.

Fortunately, long before man fell from grace, God planned that Jesus, God incarnate, who is man's original master, would buy him back from his self-imposed slavery. The truth of the matter is that practicing a religion, even a religion about Christ, does not set us free. Nor does attempted obedience to the Holy Bible set us free. Just as in the case of any slave, a person in authority must set us free, and His name is Jesus. By redefining our value and purpose, Jesus set us free from the psychological compulsion to please other people. Thus, we no longer need to live under the control of others. **Human beings are destined to be a slave to themselves and their neighbors or they will become a slave to God, through Christ.**

Jesus ended His mortal life with His arms outstretched on the cross ready to receive all who would believe and kneel before Him. He gave His life in order for us to have a direct relationship with God, Our Father. It is within this new relationship that we will come to know our true value as human beings. As born-again butterflies, we have been set free from constantly seeking the approval and favorable opinion of others. We may want the approval of others, but we no longer need it to establish that we are distinctive and valuable beings. A butterfly person, who has intrinsic value separate from his partner's opinion of him, can more easily free himself from controlling relationships and pandering behavior. A person, whose value has been determined by God, rather than one's good works or achievements, will less likely be controlled and suffer the consequences of his own pride.

As servants of God, we butterflies can now see our neighbor's value as equal to our own. Therefore, we have no further reason to put our neighbor down in order to elevate ourselves. We can stop belittling others in order to make ourselves feel relatively more special or superior. This change in perspective finally makes it possible for us to obey God's directive to love our neighbors as ourselves. We have been transformed from people, who primarily serve themselves, into people who serve others, and through our service, make the world a more functional, harmonious and peaceful place.

Without making Jesus the Lord of our lives, we are incapable of true, selfless love. As long as we see ourselves as the god of our lives, we naturally perceive other people's feelings and interests to be less valuable than our own. It is our love for Jesus that becomes the foundation for loving our neighbors. Until we first love God, our neighbors will remain our competitors, and we can never truly and unconditionally begin to love at all. Therefore, our previous caterpillar perception of love for our neighbor was nothing more than an emotional trade, not real love. **True love involves giving to another person without any expectation of a return.**

The Reality of Satan

In God's reality, life is a paradox, which is always counterintuitive to man's way of thinking. In order for God to set us free from our enslavement to ourselves, we would first have to become His slave. This is consistent with caterpillar metamorphosis. In order to be set free from the confines of a caterpillar's body, the caterpillar must submit complete control of his body, like a slave, to an unknown external force when he enters the cocoon. In the Bible, Paul refers to this in Romans 12:1, as becoming a "living sacrifice." Only when we surrender our bodies and souls to God, will He transform us into butterflies and free us from our self-centered nature and our self-indulgent way of living.

Being free has never meant becoming separated from God and living outside of His authority. We can only become truly free by living under the authority of a truly omniscient, omnipotent and benevolent God. Freedom can only be experienced beneath the umbrella of God's truth. We can never be free while we crawl in the dusty footprints of Satan's lies. God loves us. He has always had our best interests at heart. Satan, our previous master, hates God and has only had his best interests at heart. Satan, who also refused to live under God's authority, is self-centered. Therefore, all caterpillars that live in this world under his influence are self-centered, too.

Theologically and metaphorically, caterpillars, who have refused God's transformation into His image, will forever remain the immature larval, children of Lucifer, the Father of Lies. The lie he wants them to believe is that if they remain the god of their lives, the world will revolve around their needs and desires and they will be in control. If Satan can continue to make us view the world from our self-centered perspective, he will prevent us from entering into a heart-transforming, life-changing, therapeutic relationship with God. This has been the serpent's intention since Adam and Eve lived in the Garden of Eden.

In the Garden, Adam and Eve were not born as caterpillars. However, they needed to be made into caterpillars so that God could transform their descendants into butterflies. God chose Satan to do that job for Him. Satan cleverly convinced Eve that the only way to become like God was to disobey God's only rule. They became caterpillars when they ate the fruit, because in doing so, they ignored the will of God.

Many Christians do not believe that Satan is a real being. In fact, they do not believe he exists at all. They think he is a literary foil to help us understand and appreciate the goodness of God. However, God tells us that Satan is real. In fact, Jesus reinforced the true personhood of Satan when he related how He, Himself, was tempted by the devil in the desert. **If there is no Satan in the world to deceive man into believing he can be like God, then man must have chosen to be disobedient on his own. If Satan had not deceived man into living as if he was God, then mankind would be the true enemy of God.** God can forgive caterpillar people, who have been deceived and subsequently do evil, but not people who *are* evil. God defeats evil. He does not bless evil and become its benefactor. If there is no Satan, no Father of Lies, to explain the genesis of man's sinful nature, then Jesus sent His Holy Spirit to help His butterflies battle against a foe that does not exist. Without the reality of Satan, man becomes the incarnation of evil. If this is true, God could only be man's eternal adversary, not his Savior.

God created the world and everyone in it, including His angel, Satan. He became "a fallen angel" when he decided to rebel against God's authority. The reality of the "evil one" in our world is necessary to explain the origin of our sinful nature. If people do not accept the literal Biblical interpretation of the person of Satan, human beings will have no one to blame but themselves for their immoral behavior and sinful nature. If we refuse to accept Satan's existence, we negate God's gift of a psychological scapegoat to explain our dysfunctional behavior, and His entire plan for our salvation falls apart.

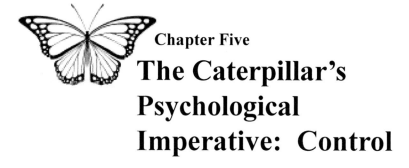

Chapter Five

The Caterpillar's Psychological Imperative: Control

And what do you benefit if you gain the whole world but are yourself lost or destroyed?

Luke 9:25 NIV

"If men were angels, no government would be necessary; if angels were to govern men neither external nor internal controls on government would be necessary."

James Madison

In my divorce recovery group, the most common complaint is that the offending spouse was extremely controlling. Some of these caterpillar spouses kept tabs on their partner's phone calls and emails. They also prevented them from seeking employment in order to remain the sole breadwinner and in control of the bank account. Sometimes, they just wanted to keep their spouses from the sexual temptations in the workplace because of the controlling spouse's own insecurity. They tended to control the couple's conversations and their social or spending agenda. Others became physically or verbally abusive in order to achieve or maintain psychological control and dominance in the relationship. Occasionally, when some were losing arguments with their spouses, they would walk off in a huff in an attempt to maintain their sense of superiority by avoiding the inevitable loss of the argument. The common thread in these broken relationships was that the perpetrators resembled self-centered caterpillars that wanted and needed to be in control. The offended spouse's most common conclusion was that their husband or wife was insecure and childish, and they compared their marital relationship to being the parent of a grown-up child.

Many of these cast-away husbands and wives thought they were marrying Christian men or women, but their spouses turned out to be posers. Some of these Christians, in name only, professed to believe in God, but they rarely went to church. However, those who did attend church did not go to church because they loved God. They went because they loved the way people thought of them, or they used the church as a business or social network. They were seeking an improved self-image, not God.

Most of these married people, either never knew or forgot that "Marriage is a covenant between a man, a woman, and God" (Malachi 2:14 NIV) and excluded Him from the marriage relationship. Those who did not want to disappoint God chose to remain in their unhealthy marriages because the Bible says "God hates divorce." (Malachi 2:16 NIV) What these long-suffering spouses did not realize is that it is impossible to disappoint God because He knows the outcome of their marriages from the beginning. God hates divorce because one spouse has turned his back on Him and the marriage, and He must seek after him. The remaining spouse is left behind broken-hearted, and He must remain to comfort him or her. God hates divorce because when one breaks the marriage covenant, each spouse, their children and their respective families will experience horrible emotional and psychological pain from the separation and divorce.

Most of these marriages lasted for years in spite of being dysfunctional because many of the spouses enabled the other spouse's addictions or infidelity, or they begrudgingly endured their spouse's wayward behavior. The offended spouses were heavily invested emotionally in their marriages and did not want them to die on the vine. Since their spouse was the most significant person in their lives, they frequently sought their partner's opinion and approval to validate their own personal worth. This co-dependent facet of their relationship allowed the dominant spouse to control the other spouse. The offended spouse had mistakenly been worshipping their marriage partner instead of God. Although many of these men and women were Christians, they were still caterpillars at heart. Their value came from man, not God. Please do not interpret this as a condemning or condescending statement regarding these men and women, for I fell right in line with them during my failed marriage.

I have heard that when we consider people of all Christian faiths, only about nine percent of all Christians hold the Christian worldview and know their true value in Christ. God's affirmative opinion of us is eternal and will never change. Unfortunately, since the other 91 percent still adhere to the secular worldview, the determination of their value is at the mercy of human beings, who can change their minds about their specialness in a heartbeat.

The Bible tells us that through one man's disobedience in the Garden of Eden, sin came into the world. As distant descendants of Adam, we are still suffering from the dysfunctional consequences of their decision. Adam and Eve badly miscalculated the effect of succumbing to Satan's temptation to become like God. They did not realize that the result of their disobedience was to be exiled from the Garden. They did not understand that there was no room in Eden for more than one God. As a consequence of losing their close relationship with their Father, they not only lost the promise of a life of everlasting in peace, harmony, and good health, they lost their unwavering confidence that God was still their advocate. Did God reject them forever, or did He merely eject them from His home? With this uncertainty looming over them, they had no assurance that they could place their hope in anyone other than themselves.

God's first two children thought that all it took to be like God was to acquire knowledge of good and evil, act as their own boss, and make their decisions without His interference. They seemed to forget that God was not only the authority figure in the Garden of Eden, He was omnipotent and omniscient, as well. They were not. In order to assume the role of God, one must be omniscient and omnipotent to serve as the final authority in the world. Adam and Eve thought that making their own decisions meant they were in control of their lives. However, it would take only a short time living outside of the Garden, before they would discover that they truly had little control over their lives, if any at all. Becoming their own bosses and making decisions independent from God was not the same as being *like* God. **The lesson we should learn from Adam and Eve is that a human being was not designed to be his own God!**

Adam and Eve may have gained the knowledge of good and evil, but losing the unlimited protection and provision of God would be greatly missed in the future. Without God's protection, they had no choice but to depend on their intellect and human strength to control their surroundings. It would be merely a matter of time before Adam and Eve and their progeny realized that human reason and intellect was inadequate to control the outside world. Without having full control of the present and the future, Adam and Eve would be forced to live in constant fear and uncertainty. Unfortunately, they had no choice, but to take control of their circumstances anyway. The more they tried to control things outside of their control, which was just about everything, the more frustrated and anxious they became.

Adam and Eve were unaware of a fundamental psychological truth that pertains to all caterpillars and butterflies. It is impossible to control anyone other than oneself. Frankly, most of us find it difficult even to do that. **Every time a person tries to control things that lie outside of his control, it leads to internal psychological conflict, frustration and ultimately anxiety.** Anxiety is the mental distress caused by fear of some person or situation that we may face in the future, but is not currently confronting us. Fear occurs when a threat lies directly before us. Fortunately, we are seldom confronted with truly dangerous and perilous situations. The emotion of anxiety is created in our minds as a result of operating without the assurance of God's power, provision and protection in our lives. Experiencing anxiety will become a way of life for all caterpillar humans. In man's attempt to predict and control his future, he has condemned himself to a life filled with fear of events that may never happen. Anxiety destroys hope and fills our lives with worry and trepidation. **In fact, there can be no real hope for human beings without understanding that God is always in control and He will never forsake us.**

The most lasting consequence of Adam and Eve's dismissal from the Garden of Eden is that human beings were forever condemned to make plans. In the Garden, they never had to make plans, for God was in control and provided all of their daily needs. Without God's provision, Adam and Eve had to make plans for their sustenance and survival. The problem with making plans is it always involves trying to predict and control the future. As we now know, trying to control something outside of our control causes people to become anxious. All human beings experience it, but it is more prevalent in caterpillars. Caterpillars behave just like Adam and Eve after the Fall. They seek to control everything: their bodies, their spouses, their neighbors, their environment and their future. Although they consciously know that it is impossible to control everything and everyone around them, they are emotionally compelled to try anyway, so they may feel safe and secure. Sadly, the more control they pursue, the more frustration and anxiety they experience. The more anxious they become, the more insecure they feel, and the more control they need to eliminate or mask their uncomfortable feelings. They are caught in the control-anxiety-control cycle. As long as they remain outside of God's protection, guidance and will, caterpillar people will more frequently suffer the deleterious, long-term psychological consequences of anxiety, worry and despair.

The method caterpillars use to quell their anxiety is to attempt to gain more control over other caterpillars and butterflies. As a result of needing control, they may try to restrict the freedoms of butterflies that know God and are not chronically anxious. When butterflies do experience anxious moments, they call upon God to help them. Butterflies know better than to try to control other people's behavior because as former caterpillars, attempting to control someone outside of their control caused or exacerbated their anxiety. They have confidence that God will eventually control all things for their benefit. So, why worry?

It is insufficient for caterpillars to overcome anxiety by merely telling themselves that they should not be anxious. It is equally ineffective to have their families, doctors, and therapists explain to them why they should not be anxious. Anxious people need a real advocate, a protector, who will never let them down. They need to know someone inherently stronger and smarter is their benefactor and is in control of their future. They need God! The only means of escape from this horrible, destructive cycle is to begin living under God's authority.

However, there are two enormous problems for caterpillars. The first is that God, or a relationship with God does not exist in their worldview. They need a butterfly to introduce them to Jesus by sharing their testimony and the Gospel with them. The second problem is that once caterpillars begin to seek the Lord, they think they can find God on their own, even though they have no idea where or how to find Him. The truth is that God must call them to Himself, and like any good shepherd, He will find his lost sheep. Only self-centered sheep could possibly believe that they could find the Good Shepherd on their own.

In today's terms, caterpillars still think they are in control and believe that all they must do is drive their bus and pick God up when they are ready. Until they understand that only God drives the bus, He will never pick them up. How afraid, anxious, depressed and dysfunctional do caterpillars have to become before they surrender the driver's seat to God? Can you imagine how much less stressful and more of an adventure life would be if they would be willing to sit in the back and let God drive?

The intense psychological desire to gain and maintain control is similar to the drug addict's physical need for a fix. He is a slave to the way the drug makes him feel and to the fear of the pain he will experience when the effects of the drug wears off. The addict's continuous need to use the drug is a conscious one designed to eliminate the anxiety of his impending withdrawal and regain control over his body. An addict's life is a twisted and tormenting way of living. In order to maintain a sense of control over his body and his life, the addict must live in an out-of control state of mind. Fear and anxiety also drives the addict to use force against others in order to secure his next fix. If the force is powerful enough, someone including themselves may become injured. It is the addict's fear and anxiety that leads to violent and criminal behavior.

A caterpillar person's need for control is similar to the addict's, but his desire is more for psychological and emotional control. His subconscious compels him to avoid a perceived painful situation or a potentially frightening event, which means the caterpillar person behaves just like a drug addict. He will wield whatever psychological or physical force necessary to get what he believes is needed to avoid pain, feel safe and secure, and resume control over his life. If his need to emotionally and psychologically manipulate others overtakes him, he and the other people involved might get hurt.

Since the caterpillar's belief that he should be in control of his life causes him emotional and psychological dysfunction, his non-God-centered worldview is obviously incorrect. If the caterpillar's worldview is wrong, then it should be no surprise that his logical conclusions about life will be wrong and, in many cases, harmful. For example, if the caterpillar's worldview leads him to believe that 2+2=5, then no matter how proficient he becomes in even the most advanced mathematics, he will always get the wrong answer. Since caterpillars have refused to allow God to complete their metamorphosis into butterflies, they remain governed by their erroneous worldview, which is contrary to God's worldview. Their unhealthy psychological perspective will lead to erroneous decision making and dysfunctional relationships. Life will be nothing more than a series of poor choices, missed opportunities, and unnecessary pain and hardship for themselves and others. By maintaining their caterpillar worldview, they will never discover God's absolute truth regarding the meaning of life and the best way to live in our world.

Since God will not transform caterpillars into butterflies against their will, caterpillars may age, but they will remain immature larvae. We butterflies have seen these wrong-thinking caterpillars mislead, deceive and corrupt the human race for thousands of years and cause turmoil and chaos in their lives and ours. If the caterpillars of our world continue to defy the authority of God during the course of their lifetime, they will not be transformed into butterflies and will never receive their new nature, the nature of God. **Not only will they never experience the abundant life and peace on Earth that God hoped for them, their need for control inevitably will result in the eradication of his neighbor's liberty and the violation of human dignity in our world.**

In all fairness to many caterpillars, they have only known reality as explained by other caterpillars that have the same frame of reference. It is as if the blind are leading the blind. Once caterpillars respond to God's call, they become transformed by placing their faith in Him. As a result, they will have new eyes to see the truth of our world from God's perspective; the truth as we butterflies know it to be; the truth for which Christ came to testify. Until that time, caterpillars will continue to be deceived by the same lie that Satan used to ruin Adam and Eve's unique relationship with God in the Garden.

We butterflies must not be impatient with our caterpillar brethren. They are not stupid or illogical. They just have not finished their metamorphosis and are incomplete. They can only see the world from their earthly perspective, which is more primitive and dysfunctional than ours. **No one, except a caterpillar, could believe that the caterpillar was to be the preferred form above the more beautiful and intricately designed, freely flying butterfly.**

Caterpillars are so intent on remaining their own god, they attempt to control everything and everyone around them. It seems impossible to convince them that they do not have to live like caterpillars anymore. They do not have to experience a lifetime of fear, anxiety, and worry that result from not having an all-powerful God to call upon when in need. Once they have been transformed by Christ, they are no longer doomed to experience controlling and abusive relationships. They can finally be free of the unnecessary pain and suffering from which caterpillar people have experienced since the beginning of time. The only thing our caterpillar friends must do to become butterflies is to stop their self-indulgent ways, lie still, place their faith in Jesus and submit themselves into God's creative hands.

In order for a caterpillar to escape his dysfunctional life, he must ask himself this question: **Which is more frightening? Living with anxiety and worry knowing he can not control everything in life, or risk giving control of his life to a God he can not see, to be transformed into something he can not imagine.** Since the definition of courage is taking action in the face of fear, then submitting to God is an act of courage, not a manifestation of weakness and helplessness, like so many nonbelievers contend. With one small mental step and one giant leap of faith, they can be transformed into butterflies and be set free from a life of selfish pursuits and the hopeless drudgery of a self-indulgent life. From our butterfly perspective, we can not understand why any caterpillar would not want God to make him or her into a butterfly!

Chapter Six
Why Only Jesus?

For, there is one God and one mediator between God and mankind, the man Christ Jesus, who gave himself as a ransom for all people. This has now been witnessed to at the proper time.

1 Timothy 2:5-6 NIV

"I have carefully examined the evidences of the Christian religion, and if I was sitting as a juror upon its authenticity I would unhesitatingly give my verdict in its favor. I can prove its truth as clearly as any proposition ever submitted to the mind of man."

Alexander Hamilton - Signer of the Declaration of Independence and Ratifier of the U.S. Constitution

I have walked you through quite a bit of psychology. So, let's review. There are only two psychological perspectives available to human beings, which I have depicted by using the metaphor of caterpillars and butterflies. Each of these perspectives on life results in a separate worldview, which results in man having two distinct natures. The first nature is a self-centered one that is common to all caterpillars. The second nature is God-centered. It is only available to caterpillar people who have surrendered control of their lives to God and have undergone their metamorphosis into butterflies. Since a caterpillar person can not *will* himself to behave like a butterfly, the only way for a person's nature to be changed is for him to voluntarily transfer the authority under which he lives, from himself to God through Christ. Once he does this, he will see the world from a new perspective, God's perspective, and his assessment of reality will change. His subsequent decisions and behavior will reflect his new worldview, and he will become a more functional human being. Although God created man, the caterpillar man is one step shy of being made into a fully functional being, the butterfly man that represents God's true image, that of Jesus Christ. God wants to finish making His caterpillars in His likeness, but each caterpillar must voluntarily respond to His call like a sheep responds to the voice of his shepherd.

I would like to continue my butterfly metaphor to present the first answer to the next question. Why Jesus? Why is it that only Jesus can transform a caterpillar into a butterfly? Why is it that only Christ can be the true God? Follow my logic. Jesus, unlike all other humans, including all of the ancient prophets, did His Father's will perfectly. Therefore, he could not merely have been a mortal caterpillar man that was transformed into a butterfly because even the most mature butterfly can not do God's will perfectly. Since only God can do His own will perfectly, and Jesus fulfilled God's will perfectly, then Jesus must be God. Finally, since neither a caterpillar nor a butterfly can ever create a new butterfly by themselves, then only God can make a butterfly. Since Jesus is God, then only Jesus can transform a caterpillar into a butterfly.

There are also five theological and Biblical reasons why Jesus was the incarnation of God, and can be the only one to whom we can entrust our lives. The first reason is that Jesus had the essence of the Father in Him at his birth, which is consistent with Biblical account of Mary's Immaculate Conception. Secondly, there are numerous prophetic passages in the Bible predicting Christ's birth, and there were many witnesses to Christ's crucifixion and resurrection. Thirdly, Jesus was the only religious figure who claimed He was God. Fourthly, our faith in Jesus is justified because we have proof that he had the greatest love for us because He voluntarily sacrificed His own life for us. Finally, Jesus is the only deity who wanted to have a relationship with us. In fact, He promised us a direct relationship with Him by sending His Spirit to live within us as a sign of His sincerity. He was willing to make a new covenant with us and sealed the deal with His own blood. Jesus proved to us by His actions, including His death on the cross, that He will never forsake His relationship with us.

The next two explanations for why Jesus is God are purely practical. We can only have a relationship with a live person. We can not have a relationship with dead prophets, inanimate objects, or a set of religious rules or a mystical force. In Christ's case, we have Biblical and non-Biblical accounts of His resurrection to reassure us that He is alive. However, even the knowledge that God is alive may still not be enough to gain our trust and accept him as our Savior. We must also be assured that He experienced human living and succeeded in overcoming human pitfalls and temptations, before we will consider placing our faith in Him. Only Jesus meets these requirements.

However, the best answer to why Jesus is the only one who could transform us into butterflies is more than metaphorical or theological. It is psychological. This answer does not depend on one's religious belief or special understanding of the Scriptures. My logic is as follows and begins with this example. Imagine we needed the services of a plastic surgeon or a psychiatrist. We must trust this person before we will allow him to cut into our bodies to resurface or enhance us, or delve into our past to resolve any emotional or psychiatric issues that afflict us. We can not learn to trust this person unless we can get to know him well enough, and we can not get to know him well enough without checking his references and talking to him several times. Therefore, if we need to know our doctors well enough to trust them with our bodies for a limited amount of time, how much more trust must we have in God to let Him have control over our entire lives? We must be able to develop a deep, intimate, and long-lasting relationship with God in order to know and trust Him well enough to relinquish more and more control of our lives to Him. Finally, there is one more extremely important thing to consider. We can not develop a relationship with anyone, even God, if God does not want to develop a relationship with us.

Jesus welcomes a relationship with anyone who accepts Him as their Lord and Savior. In fact, he died to make Himself available to all who would believe.

There are a few more reasons to explain, "Why Jesus?" We will never trust anyone with our lives unless we are absolutely certain that this person will always place our interests above his own, even to the point of sacrificing His life for us. Only then, will we ever trust Him enough to pledge our entire lives to Him. Jesus is the only living being who fulfills all of the above prerequisites. He wanted us to know His immense love for us and how much He values us. He also wanted to relate to us as our Father. He wanted us to trust Him like little children who desire to grow up to be just like Dad. Jesus wanted us to have faith in Him and place our lives in His hands, so He could finish making each of His precious caterpillars into His likeness, a butterfly. These are the reasons why only Jesus can make a butterfly!

To God's dismay, many caterpillar people have ignored or rejected His Son, Jesus, and have chosen to become Atheists, Humanists or Darwinists. Unlike butterflies, they believe human beings evolved as a result of random chance. Therefore, people possess no intrinsic value and their purpose is limited to self-fulfillment and survival. They think that being a caterpillar is all they were intended to be.

Since people have a natural desire to know their origins, how do caterpillars attempt to learn the truth about themselves, their past and their future? They are condemned to spend most of their adult lives searching the past. Geologists, biologists, archeologists, physicists, cosmologists, and geneticists must dig up the earth, examine their living and dead samples under the microscope, and use their telescopes to search the universe in an attempt to learn the answer to life's most compelling questions. Human beings have spent centuries trying to determine how life began, the purpose and meaning of life, and what lies ahead for them. Generations of men have spent their entire lives pursuing this never-ending quest and died without discovering the answers to these questions. What a shame!

If these science-worshipping caterpillars had responded to God's call and found the courage to submit to His authority, they could have discovered their previous man-centered, scientific understanding of life was incomplete at best or totally false at worst. Man does have intrinsic value and a divine purpose in life. They would have realized that their search for the answers to these transcendent human questions were unattainable through human effort. They could have chosen to become butterflies that were directly told the truth by God, through His Word, The Bible, regarding the meaning of life and their noble purpose and glorious future. Only butterflies that have experienced an intimate encounter with their Creator during their own transformation can be certain that God has a plan and a future for them. In tough times, only butterflies can be truly comforted in the everlasting arms of God. Only butterflies can be confident of their eternal future in Heaven as they take their last breath. What a blessing!

Human beings must place their faith in God before He reveals life's truth to them, not learn the truth, so they can place their faith in God. We can only develop a functional worldview by placing our lives in God's hands, so He can give us a new perspective on life. Jesus does not want us to believe in Him merely to be worshipped. He wants us to worship Him because it is the only way to make us psychologically healthy and functional. He does not want us to follow Him just because it is the **right** thing to do. He wants us to follow Him because it is the **smart** thing to do. He has an incredible adventure planned for us and He wants us to experience the abundant and peaceful life He promised us. However, He will not take us on Life's Adventure unless we fire ourselves as the leader of the pack and follow Him. Although God pursues and calls us, He designed us to first respond to His call in order to receive His most precious gift, Himself, The Truth! To know Christ is to know the Truth, and knowing the Truth, not learning the truth, is the only way for man to know the meaning and purpose of life.

The Psychological Pitfalls of Not Knowing Jesus

Knowing the Truth, Jesus Christ, changes our worldview, so we can see the world from God's perspective. The psychological benefit of changing our worldview is that when we change our role in life from being god to surrendering to God, we develop a new nature. Changing from a caterpillar into a butterfly is like changing from a child into and adult. The Apostle Paul makes a reference to this in 1 Corinthians 13:11 (NLT). He writes, "When I was a child, I spoke and thought as a child. But when I grew up, I put away childish things." Because we are born as caterpillars, we see ourselves and our world through our immature caterpillar eyes, and like all children, we place ourselves at the center of our world. In other words, Paul is saying that as we grow up, we are to put away our childish notion that life is about us and outgrow our self-centered perspective that defined our caterpillar childhood.

Unfortunately, as long as a caterpillar remains a caterpillar, he will be unable to change his child-like perspective on life regardless of his age. If an adult continues to reason and behave like a child, he will adversely affect everyone with whom he comes in contact, just like he did when he *was* a child. Let me drive my point home by describing a scene that is familiar to all of us who are parents or care for children.

A two year old child has been sitting in a room for a short time happily playing with several different toys scattered on the floor around him. He has a toy in each hand when another child his age walks in holding a different toy. Can you guess what the child with all the toys does? He sees the other child holding a new toy, walks over to him and grabs the toy out of his hand, leaving that child in tears. The first child walked away with the toy, and he seemed oblivious of the fact that he upset the other child and made him cry. This overtly selfish behavior is so common among children that people respond by saying, "kids will be kids" and consider this behavior to be "just human nature." This child was not taught to be selfish. It came naturally to him.

As a facilitator in my church's divorce recovery ministry, I have witnessed this same childish behavior in adults. Imagine this same child, who was playing with all his toys, forty years later as a fully grown man. Assuming he has not developed a God-centered, butterfly worldview by surrendering his life to Christ, he is now just a 42 year-old caterpillar. He may be smarter and more experienced in the ways of the world, but he is still a caterpillar. Assume, he has been married for fourteen years, and he has three children. A few months ago he noticed a beautiful young woman at work. He started a casual, seemingly harmless relationship with her. In a few months, he believes he has fallen in love with her and decides to leave his wife and family to begin a long-term relationship with the intent of marrying this new woman. Certainly, this man is mature by worldly standards, but he still responds to his urges and desires as he did when he was two years old. He noticed a new toy (the new woman) he liked more than his current toys (his wife and family) that he had been playing with for 14 years and left them all for the "new toy" that seemed more intriguing to him. He left his family (his old toys) in a heap on the floor, just as he abandoned his old toys forty years ago when he snatched away the other child's toy.

To the outside observer, it seems that he could have cared less about his family's feelings or the emotional damage they will suffer for many years to come. It was as if he became deaf to his wife and children's cries of grief and blind to their tears. It is difficult for a caterpillar person to see the pain he is causing his family because the focus of his life usually is on himself and his new toy. Although he is a middle-aged adult, he made a self-centered decision and behaved just like he did when he was a two-year old child. He may be bigger and more accomplished, but he still looks and acts like a caterpillar to me. **Without entering into a relationship with Jesus, regardless how old and experienced a caterpillar becomes, he will remain an immature larva imprisoned in his self-centered world.**

Since a caterpillar's significance depends on the opinion and approval of other people, his proclivity for causing pain and discord in relationships escalates when he feels stressed, weak or inadequate. He will be drawn into nearly any situation or relationship that will bolster his level of esteem. A caterpillar is more likely to cheat on his wife because he does not have enough willpower to overcome his need for approval and validation that might be gained from a relationship with the other woman. Employing his own willpower to quench his burning sexual desire for another woman is like a person, whose pants are on fire trying to run fast enough to blow out the flames. Eventually, he will run out of his own power, collapse and be consumed by the flames of his own desire. If you have ever seen a caterpillar run, you know this method of extinguishing a fire is doomed to fail.

Any caterpillar that lives for himself lives without the power of God behind him. He will inevitably be overwhelmed by his unhealthy urges and selfish desires. Even immature butterflies may succumb to sexual temptation and get burned in this world. However, a butterfly has the desire to be obedient to God and possesses the wings needed to escape the heat and smoke of what was a hellish decision. Regardless of the number of legs a caterpillar has, he can not move fast enough to escape the fire that burns within him. Not only will he get burned time and time again during his lifetime, a caterpillar that rejects Christ's invitation to be transformed, condemns himself to experience these same flames in Hell for eternity. Until all caterpillars become butterflies that adopt God's Biblical worldview, their evil nature can never be eradicated. They will be unable to obey God's command to flee sexual temptation. **The ability to free ourselves from our childish, self-centered nature, which exists in all human caterpillars, is not a matter of maturation. It is a matter of transformation.**

In the case of this unfaithful man, who knowingly hurt his family, he will probably lose the respect of his children and those in the community. He may become remorseful, endure emotional pain or suffer from poor health as a consequence of his adultery. He may incur legal and considerable financial consequences as a result of his infidelity and divorce. He may harbor guilt and shame that will ultimately erode his own self-image and sabotage his future relationships. Instead of behaving like a responsible husband and father, he behaved just as he did when he was a child. He wanted what he wanted, and he wanted it now, and he did not care who got hurt in the process. **There is a psychological principle that is universal to all human beings: When we purposefully behave in a way that hurts another person, we will inevitably hurt ourselves.**

One would think that, as a fully grown man, he would have stopped acting like a child, and become a more responsible adult who could delay or deny his need for immediate gratification. Unfortunately, he never gave up his childish perspective on life. He continued to live as if he was the center of his own existence. Any person who believes that life revolves around him expects to get his way all the time. In order for a child to give up his childish ways, he must be taught occasionally to say "no" when it comes to satisfying many of his desires and urges. He must learn to delay gratification in order to become psychologically healthy and live a functional life. If an adult has not learned to delay gratification as a child, he will have difficulty learning it as an adult. Even if caterpillars believe in God, it will be difficult for them to have hope in God because the hardest thing about having hope is delaying our desire to seek gratification on our own. If we can not wait for God to prepare the way to give us our heart's desire, then we can never experience God's promise of hope and a future. The truth is that since a caterpillar does not believe God has a hand in controlling his future, he only has hope in himself to control the future and achieve successful outcomes. **Since caterpillars can not control the future, they can never have hope at all. Only butterflies can truly have hope!**

Self-centeredness is the natural state of all caterpillars and is the source of all evil towards their fellow man. A grown man, who leaves his wife and family is committing an evil act, yet he rationalizes his decision by telling himself rational lies that are consistent with his self-centered perspective on life. He, consciously or subconsciously, believes his decision to abandon his family will serve his best psychological and emotional interests. As long as a person remains a caterpillar, he will eventually put his needs and desires ahead of the best interests of his wife and family regardless how much he says he loves them. Any caterpillar man may fail to maintain his moral code if he has a powerful psychological need for personal validation or distraction from the stresses and responsibilities of life. Unlike butterflies, caterpillars do not have an abiding love for God. Without love for God, caterpillars can not maintain their promise of fidelity, because their desire to please themselves will usually take precedence over any thoughts they might have about obeying and pleasing God.

Even a strong religious devotion is not enough for a caterpillar to avoid temptation. All of us have heard stories about members of the clergy who have been unfaithful to their spouses. The scandal usually results in the destruction of their families and the loss of their position in the church. It is apparent that not every religious leader has adopted God's Biblical worldview and lives accordingly. It takes more than practicing a religion to prevent a person from committing adultery because being religious does not change a person's self-centered worldview. Surprisingly, the divorce rate is nearly the same for believers as the general population because only a small percentage of Christians and Catholics have totally surrendered their will to God and become immersed in the functional Biblical worldview. A person has to be committed to living under God's authority in order to obey God's command to flee sexual temptation.

Unless a person believes that pleasing God always precedes satisfying his own desires, he will emotionally be compelled to do whatever he believes will satisfy his needs, even if it places his own future in jeopardy. The problem with a caterpillar that repeatedly needs to earn his significance is that he is more likely to make his decisions based on his feelings rather than his reasoning ability. He has no long-term plan to earn his psychological significance. He merely responds many times per day to a series of internal emotional needs.

Let us return to the caterpillar man who left his wife and family for another woman. He violated several of The Ten Commandments and sinned against God. He betrayed his neighbors, who in this case were his wife and family. God claimed that a husband and wife were to become one flesh. Therefore, any pain he caused his wife by his self-centered actions would eventually cause him pain. Caterpillars are selfish and short-sighted like children. They tend only to see the benefits of their choices, not the pitfalls. Due to their immature perspective on life, they are easily deceived regarding the consequences of their behavior. Metaphorically, it is as if these caterpillars live within such dense, dark foliage, they can not see the predator that is prowling like a lion right before them. Subsequently, they develop a false sense of safety. They are so busy satisfying their lustful appetites, they are oblivious to the danger in which their self-serving behavior has placed them. Not only will they fail to flee sexual immorality, they will be devoured by their lust and will not realize it until it is too late. If only this caterpillar man believed that he was accountable to God and was to serve according to God's pleasure, not his own. He would desire to do whatever God commands in order to avoid hurting himself and those he loves. Becoming an old caterpillar does not guarantee that he will have the wisdom and will-power to behave honorably.

I have learned over the years that if spouses are not willing to place the interests of the Creator of the Universe ahead of their own, the likelihood that they will place their partner's interests consistently ahead of their own is nearly zero. Subconsciously, every person about to be married wants his or her partner to possess the character of Jesus. They will never have to worry about infidelity or that they will be forsaken for something or someone else. In fact, they can be assured that their husband or wife will not only support them and their family, they will raise their children in the admonition of the Lord and will lay down their lives for their family should the occasion arise. It takes a God-centered butterfly person to be able to consistently put his spouse and his family's needs above his own desires.

We must remember that even a butterfly man is not Christ. He is merely made in His likeness. He is not perfect. Sexual temptation is so compelling that even some less mature butterflies may succumb to it. Yes, even butterfly people, who are still working out their salvation in fear and trembling, can be tempted into sinful behavior. However, unlike caterpillars, they will be able to invoke the power of the Holy Spirit to help them in their psychological and emotional struggle to avoid their dysfunctional and potentially destructive behavior. They also might think twice about dragging the Holy Spirit into being an eye-witness to their sinful escapades. The butterfly has the advantage of being internally governed by the love he has for God, while the caterpillar is only externally governed by the fear of being caught. Butterflies can flee before they commit the sin. Caterpillar people behave like roaches when the light of truth exposes them. They do not fall on bended knees and beg for forgiveness. They crawl away from the light and hide from the consequences of their sinful behavior. The Holy Spirit counsels butterflies before the betrayal. Caterpillars will require man's counseling afterwards. When butterflies do sin, they can receive God's forgiveness and have His support in their recovery. The caterpillar man must wait for the offended caterpillar spouse to forgive him. Good luck with that!

Caterpillars are unaware of God's counsel and forgiveness. Since they do not have a relationship with God through Christ because they have rejected God's call, how can they ever expect to be forgiven by God? How could they ever truly believe God will help them recover from their immoral or immature choices if they have refused to capitulate to His authority? They can not. Without a true belief that God is their benefactor, they can only mentally rationalize forgiveness. They can never know in their heart of hearts that they were truly forgiven, which leaves them with a restless spirit and an unsettled conscience. Lack of forgiveness may adversely affect their self-image for years to come, if not the rest of their lives. This does not mean that God does not intervene in a caterpillar's life. In fact, just the opposite is true. God intervenes in every caterpillar's life, for He is continually calling and inviting him to become one of His butterflies while he is still a self-centered, sinner pretending to be his own god.

The Benefits of Knowing Jesus

In order to please God, a person must seek to do God's will, not his own. Before he can fulfill God's will, he must surrender authority of his life to Jesus, which automatically fulfills God's First Commandment: thou shall have no other God before Him. Once a person makes God number one in his life, he will have little trouble obeying the next three Commandments. If he truly loves God with all of his heart, mind and strength, he will be truly able to love his neighbor. As he becomes a more mature follower of Jesus, his natural human inclination towards murder, adultery, stealing, bearing false witness against his neighbor, or coveting his neighbor's wife and property will melt away like a caterpillar's skin does in the cocoon. Only a butterfly, who believes that he and his neighbor are valued equally by God, will desire to obey God's instructions and be capable of loving his neighbor as himself.

If the unfaithful husband in my previous example becomes a butterfly, he can see life from God's perspective and accept the truth of God's wisdom. He can foresee the pain that will come to him and his wife as a consequence of committing adultery or participating in other harmful sexual activities. If a man views his wife from God's perspective, he will see her as a gift from God. If he desires to please God more than himself, he will respect and appreciate that gift, and he will be less likely to commit adultery. When a man sees his family's interests as important as his own, he will not put his interests ahead of his family if he realizes it will be at their expense.

When a man loves Jesus and lives for kingdom purposes rather than worldly ones, he will know that worldly pleasures can not compare to the tremendous feeling he gets from knowing and pleasing God. When a man has surrendered his life to Christ, God determines his value to be equal to the life of His Son. When a man loves God and knows his true value, he will have less need for the affirmation of another person to make him feel special and more significant. Therefore, defying God's will for his marriage is much less likely to occur. Once a man commits himself to God, the ability to keep his commitment to his wife will occur more easily. God equips a transformed man with the character traits needed to find joy in his marriage and all of his relationships. He will not settle for periods of fleeting pleasure or happiness found in the temporary circumstances of our world. **Developing the worldview and nature of God allows man to develop more faithful, enduring marriages and harmonious relationships.**

When a butterfly lives his life God's way, he will live the most functional and rewarding life possible. He will finally understand the true meaning of life and man's existence on Earth. In the first part of John 14:6, Jesus proclaimed that "I am the Way ...." This means that:

- living under Christ's authority is the only *Way* to have the abundant life God planned for us,

- living under Christ's authority is the only *Way* we can learn the truth about our world, our intrinsic value and purpose, understand the magnitude of God's love for us, and experience the greatest joy in our relationships,
- living under Christ's authority is the only *Way* we can ever experience the eternal life He promised.

When we do not live under God's control, we tend to live out of control. When we allow God to be the true Lord of our lives, instead of ourselves, then and only then, can we experience true love and maximum joy in our lives. Christ's goal was to change us from orphaned, wayward people, (caterpillars) who never knew their true Father, into His children (butterflies). He transformed us from self-centered people who lived to be served, into servants of God who love and serve Him and His people. He wanted to change us from fallen people condemned to scratch out a life in the earth into people with a chance for a new and abundant life on Earth.

Living as our own god leads to eternal separation, not only from God's power, blessings, and wisdom, but from God, Himself. Once God transforms a willing caterpillar person into a butterfly, God's goal of making that person in His image is on the road to completion. It took a few thousand years before God through Christ made His first caterpillar into a butterfly, but to God a thousand years is but a day. He wants to change us from being the source of evil in the world into being the mediators of God's love, peace and good will. **Only when all caterpillars become butterflies that worship the only one true God through Christ, can His proclamation "*Joy to the World*" come true and His completed creation begin to experience "*Peace on Earth as it is in Heaven.*"**

We butterflies are extremely grateful to Jesus for saving us from ourselves. Unfortunately, we are mute to express our gratitude to God. Imagine billions of born-again butterflies on Earth and in Heaven assembled to worship God. We praise Him by raising our spectacular wings in silence, as only butterflies can, and perform a wave in such perfect harmony and humility that it gives glory to God. Our Heavenly Father would see this humble display and say again, "Let us make man in our image" and Jesus would turn to the Father and reply, "It is finished!" They lovingly gazed upon their growing family of completed, authentic, peaceful **butterfly** men and women, and God saw that it was very good.

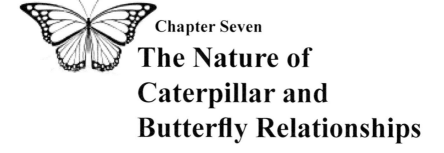

Chapter Seven

The Nature of Caterpillar and Butterfly Relationships

*Do nothing out of selfish ambition or vain conceit. Rather,
in humility value others above yourselves, not looking to
your laws. All the miseries and evil men suffer from vice,
crime, ambition, injustice, oppression, slavery, and war
proceed own interests but each of you to the interests of
the others. In your relationships with one another, have the
same mindset as Christ Jesus.*

Philippians 2:3-5

*"The moral principles and precepts contained in
the Scripture ought to form the basis of all our civil
constitutions and from their despising or neglecting the
precepts contained in the Bible."*

Noah Webster

Our self-centered, secular culture promotes the notion of rugged
individualism and self-reliance. In reality, this worldly concept of
self-reliance is a complete myth. In America, the average person
stops for coffee already made for him, pulls in to a service station
for gas, and picks up his dry cleaning before he gets to work in
the morning. Having other people provide us with goods and
services can hardly be called self-reliance. The truth is that God
designed man in His image, and just as He has an interdependent
relationship with His triune community of three, God expects
people to live in community and be dependent upon each other. He

created man to be a social person, who enters into relationships, consciously or subconsciously, with the goal of satisfying his need for companionship, intimacy and community.

God gave his caterpillars and butterflies the mandate to provide for themselves and their families. However, without a relationship with God, caterpillars replaced the provision of God with the illusion of self-reliance and self-sufficiency. This notion developed because they understood God to be self-sufficient, which He is. Biblically speaking, caterpillars believed Satan's lie that they could be like God. They live under the false notion that they are functioning independently of any God, when the truth of the situation is that they have just replaced the true God with themselves. The consequence of seeing themselves as the lord of their lives is that, subconsciously, they consider their fellow human beings to be subservient and intrinsically less valuable than themselves. This imagined inequality serves as the foundation for all of their relationships. People who see themselves as the primary person in their lives condemn themselves to participate in psychologically unequal relationships. **They will be competitors rather than partners and will experience more conflict and turmoil as each one battles for control. This psychological competition will cause people to experience less peaceful, meaningful and fulfilling relationships in life. This is Satan's curse on the caterpillar man!**

The New Testament reveals to us that when we accept Christ as our new God, He sends the Holy Spirit to partner with us to battle against the wily Satan, who is constantly enticing us back towards self-worship. **Essentially, a butterfly's life is a constant internal psychological struggle between serving himself and God.** The more the Holy Spirit prevails within us, the more often we win the battle. The less we see ourselves as the god of our lives, the more we see ourselves as God's servants. Once we accept becoming His servant, we can better see our neighbor, who we used to see as our servant, as our equal. Psychologically, this new equality allows us to assess their interests to be as important as our own, and when necessary, place their needs ahead of our own. **People who serve each other do not control each other. Therefore, they can have more peaceful relationships and experience a more joyful and meaningful life. This is God's blessing for the butterfly man!** Being a follower of Christ is difficult, not easy. It takes discipline and perseverance, but it is the *smart* way to go through life. Only when a person becomes a butterfly, can he see a problem or dilemma from God's perspective and make the moral and less destructive choice.

Generally, it is within God-centered relationships that we find our greatest joy in life, and it is joy, not happiness that will provide us our best feelings in life. The good feelings of happiness are a product of circumstances, situations, or happenings, which are always transient. Joy is the warm, satisfied feeling we find in relationships in which people see each other as having equal value. Caterpillars can also experience joyful times in life. However, they are usually transient because the caterpillar's need to be in control inevitably disrupts the psychological balance of power, which causes them to dominate or control the relationship. Joy is most frequently experienced in God-centered relationships that can remain more equally balanced.

True partnerships can remain strong, rewarding, and enduring in the midst of the most dangerous or miserable conditions. For example, in prisoner of war camps people found the will to live because they still found strength and meaning in their existing relationships, which helped them persevere. The prisoners owned nothing and possessed little, so materialism could not interfere with the development of their relationships. Ironically, they had to be treated like slaves for them to escape the world's gravitational pull towards materialism and self-indulgence. After the guards stripped these prisoners of their belongings, all that remained were the relationships with their fellow inmates, which sustained them through their ordeal.

In the Gospel story, Jesus told a wealthy man that in order to enter the kingdom of Heaven he would have to leave everything he owned behind. Jesus did not imply that being impoverished was the key to entering Heaven. It was that man's possessions and his materialistic worldview interfered with his relationship with God and his neighbors. Jesus said, "No one can serve two masters. Either he will hate the one and love the other, or he will be devoted to the one and despise the other…" (Matt 6:24 NIV) This was not just a statement of fact. This established the parameters for healthy human relationships and joyful living. We can not serve God while worshipping wealth, and at the same time, expect to develop or maintain an intimate relationship with Him. Also, it is impossible to serve ourselves and our neighbors at the same time and expect our human relationships to flourish. If our relationship with God is solid, we will have more love to offer our family and friends. When we have the knowledge that God is for us and protects us, we can allow ourselves to become more emotionally vulnerable, which is necessary to deepen our relationships. **To be made in God's likeness means becoming a relational human being. Man's greatest joy in life is always derived from his relationships.**

On the other hand, even the best caterpillar relationships are self-serving in nature, and true, lasting partnerships are less probable. It should be no surprise that caterpillars involved in a psychological competition with other caterpillars and butterflies would trigger interpersonal conflicts. Inevitably, someone in the relationship will get neglected, stepped on, or trampled. **Caterpillar relationships eventually become competitions to achieve psychological control at best, or become adversarial, abusive and destructive at their worst when one participant develops the psychological need to become totally dominant.**

I often hear people in relationships say that the other person is controlling them. Well, they may be correct. It is the caterpillar's nature to be in control. However, the controlled person also must be held somewhat accountable for creating or remaining in their controlling relationship. That person is also competing with his partner for control in an attempt to maintain or regain his own significance. He just happens to be losing. He becomes a victim of his own nature, which dictates that his sense of specialness and significance depends on the opinion and approval of the other person. Unknowingly, he places himself under the other person's control. Caterpillars are a slave to their nature, and as long as they remain caterpillars, they will be unable to escape it. This dysfunctional way of living is a natural product of a caterpillar's self-centered worldview and is a terrible way to go through life.

Unfortunately, relationships between two self-centered caterpillars, a caterpillar and a butterfly, or two immature butterflies can still be extremely selfish, hurtful and destructive. The more we seek to serve ourselves, the more difficult it becomes to have satisfying and enduring relationships. The more selfless we become, the more rewarding will be our relationships.

Most of our emotional distress and feelings of inferiority and insecurity result from our dysfunctional relationships. This distress is worse for caterpillars because the methods they employ to alleviate the pain and stress derived from their unhealthy relationships results in even more distress and dysfunction in their relationships. Let's consider a married couple, John and Judy. John and Judy had a terrible fight. Instead of persevering to resolve the issue, John went to a bar angry and frustrated. He stayed for hours and drank too much in an attempt to numb his guilt, pain or anger. The alcohol may have lowered his inhibitions to such and extent that he could have hooked up with another woman, lost his money gambling or became so impaired that he could have had a car accident on the way home; all of which would probably be more destructive to his marriage than the argument itself.

When John finally returns home to his wife, there will probably be another, even more volatile argument, which will evoke in him even more pain and guilt. It would not be unlikely that John would use the same method of dealing with his frustrations and find himself back at the bar. John is trying to deal with his distressing emotions of anger, guilt, shame or despair by removing himself from the conflict. Instead of finishing the argument with his wife or defusing the conflict by admitting he was wrong, he chose to mask his feelings with alcohol and distract himself by involving himself in other destructive behaviors. Remember, caterpillars can not afford to lose an argument because their sense of superior significance might be challenged or destroyed.

In order to help John resolve the issue with Judy at the time of the argument, He needed to be able to call upon an expert for immediate advice and guidance. If we rule out an emergency 3 a.m. house call or phone consultation with a psychologist, the only other person who fits this description is God. However, John is a caterpillar, and he has no existing relationship with God, so he has no other god to turn to than himself. If John was the guilty party, it would have been unlikely that he would have admitted his fault and asked for forgiveness. A person, who sees himself as the lord of his life, does not ask forgiveness of an underling. If his wife hurt John's feelings as a result of the conflict, he would need to seek comfort. Unfortunately, John did not have God to comfort him and a distraught or guilty man can not comfort himself. His only option is to mask or escape his emotional pain or guilt.

Since John never stood in humility before God, it is unlikely that he would admit his errors and transgressions to his wife. He had no experience repenting and confessing his sins before God, so he will be less capable of saying he was sorry to defuse the argument. However, while intoxicated at 3 a.m., John is more likely to find comfort and understanding in the arms of another woman, which would make his life go from bad to worse.

John's strategy was to escape or mask the emotional pain of his dysfunctional relationship. His life evolved into an unending cycle of emotional pain followed by dysfunctional and destructive behavior resulting in more emotional pain, which prompted more unhealthy behavior. The result of this cycle is that his marriage will be dominated by interpersonal conflicts, which will create psychological stress that leads to more anxiety, fear, and worry. **Remember, that it is a caterpillar's self-centered nature that compels him to get his own way, and it is his constant need to reinforce his significance that drives this horrible cycle that is common to every caterpillar and immature butterfly.** Ironically, the caterpillar that worships his intellect and prides himself on his superior reasoning ability usually makes his decisions based on his emotions.

This pattern of behavior is no surprise to us butterflies because we now know that it is our intimate relationship with God, not our intellect that subdues our fear, anxiety, and pride that governed us as caterpillars. Without the help and counsel of God, man becomes a slave to his pride and his need to be right all the time. The man who exists without God, resorts to his own counterproductive methods of coping with pain and other distressing emotions. Who else can he call upon? If he had relied on God, he could have found comfort and solace in prayer before he acted. During the argument, he could have called on this bit of wisdom in God's Word, "A gentle answer turns away wrath, but a harsh word stirs up anger." (Proverbs 15:1, NIV) He could have obeyed God's command to forgive his wife or ask for forgiveness. Unfortunately, if one does not know God, one is lost in these situations. The caterpillar thinks the three magic words in a marriage are "I love you." A butterfly knows the three magic words are "I was wrong" or "Please forgive me."

The psychological value of having a relationship with God is that we can direct our attention towards God and away from ourselves and the person with whom we are in conflict. When we seek God, we move from trying to lessen or avoid our pain to finding comfort and peace. Our psychological focus changes from masking our pain to seeking God's guidance for the resolution of the conflict and the restoration of harmony in our tumultuous relationship. The follower of Christ sees pain as a signal that requires God's care and wisdom. The self-centered person interprets pain as something to be avoided or eliminated at all costs. Little does the caterpillar man know that every time he tries to eliminate emotional pain through his own devices, he will inflict more pain on himself and everyone involved.

Much of man's emotional and physical suffering is the product of his selfish behaviors which range from thoughtlessness, to neglect, to abuse, to immorality, to criminality, to homicide and suicide, to war and finally genocide. Certainly, caterpillars experience periods of peace and harmony in their relationships, but when they, subconsciously or consciously, feel compelled to establish or reinforce their superior position in the relationship, their self-centered nature will call them into action. They will exert their will to get their way in order to reassure themselves that they are still the lord of their lives. During these times of conflict and confrontation, their brains seem to stop functioning. They tend to block out or ignore how their upcoming speech will adversely affect the other person or persons. They become oblivious to the effect their behavior will have on others, and they usually will live to regret their actions and pay dearly for their harsh words. Caterpillars that believe they have the primary status in the relationship feel compelled to win fights and arguments regardless how minor. Subconsciously, it increases their significance and restores their image as the supreme authority in their lives. They may strut off after a conflict as if they were victorious, but, subconsciously, the guilt over their mistreatment of the other person will slowly and inevitably erode their self-image. **Unlike butterflies that seek to fix problems, caterpillars seek to fix blame because when they can put another person down, it falsely elevates their sense of importance and reassures them of their superior status.**

Butterfly Relationships

All butterflies have God's Spirit in them, but they still retain their innate, sinful caterpillar spirit. The advantage of having the Holy Spirit within them is they have immediate access to the power of His Spirit and wisdom to help them fight against their congenital, self-centered spirit. In the process of their transformation, butterflies had God's nature transplanted in them. Unfortunately, they will never be perfectly disciplined in controlling or changing their destructive impulses dictated by their old nature. However, the more they empty themselves of their sense of self-importance, the greater the Holy Spirit grows within the butterfly person. The more closely the butterfly's nature resembles the personality and character of Jesus, the more gracious, forgiving, merciful and loving towards other butterflies and caterpillars he becomes.

In order for God to transform a caterpillar into a butterfly, the caterpillar must proclaim Jesus to be his new God. As a result of his profession of faith, he tacitly renounces himself as his own god. Now, he has no further need to maintain the pretense of his god-like image, so it is unnecessary for him to always prevail in his day to day relational conflicts. He no longer feels compelled to defeat his partner or friend, because his significance no longer depends on being the victor.

Unlike caterpillars, butterflies understand that an argument is a means of resolving an issue, not re-establishing their position of power in the relationship. They have learned that peace and harmony is the goal in life, not winning meaningless battles with their partner. Butterflies would rather defuse the situation by saying they are sorry or admit they were wrong, so they can restore peace and find contentment in reconciling the relationship. Butterflies are God-centered people who choose to employ God's wisdom, so they will cause less harm to their partner and their relationships. Power and control are no substitutes for the wisdom of peace making. "Blessed are the peacemakers, for they shall be called sons of God." (Matt. 5:9, NIV) Butterflies are born-again sons and daughters of God.

Because butterflies see themselves as servants of God, their primary desire for their relationships differs from caterpillars. **Butterflies want to get right with God, whereas caterpillars want to be right because they see themselves as god.** Once butterflies have surrendered control of their lives to God, the desire to have their own way all of the time decreases since they no longer see themselves as the primary person in their lives. Their point of view changes and they begin to see themselves and others as equal servants of God, rather than competing caterpillars trying to have all the leaves for themselves. **Once a caterpillar lets God transform him into the likeness of Jesus, he will discover that his best feeling in life comes from serving, not being served.** Man's nature has now been changed from that of a master into a servant.

As butterflies mature, their nature will more closely resemble the image of Jesus, and they will be able to exhibit true sacrificial love more frequently in their relationships. Since butterflies must no longer earn their neighbor's approval as a measure of their significance, they do not need to manipulate and use them. Finally, God-centered butterflies can approach their relationships based on what they can offer others, rather than what they can extract from them. **The hallmark of the God-centered, butterfly relationship is love and support, not competition and control.**

The Ten Commandments and the Nature of God

God knew that it was necessary to have a properly oriented relationship with Him before we could have healthy and joyful relationships with others. This truth is evident in the Ten Commandments, which are God's rules for all of our relationships. God gave them to Moses in a specific order because it reflected an order of importance to God. Obeying the First Commandment is necessary to obey the next four, which tell us how to relate to our Heavenly Father and our Earthly parents. The next five tell us how to relate to our neighbors. If we can not obey the ones pertaining to God and our parents, it will be impossible to consistently obey the ones pertaining to our neighbors.

In order for butterflies to achieve truly loving relationships with their neighbors, they have to follow God's prescription in the Bible, which begins with making Christ the Lord of their lives. For us to complete our transformation into the image of Jesus, we have to follow His treatment plan, so we could enjoy peaceful and harmonious relationships with others. His plan is quite simple! **Love God first. Then, we will be able to love our neighbor as ourselves. We can not be both self-centered caterpillars and neighbor-centered butterflies at the same time.**

After we fire ourselves as the god of our lives and live under the authority of the one true God, He replaces our self-centered worldview with His own, so we can see the absolute truth regarding the reality of man's existence on Earth. This reality is not true merely because, among all of the deities that men worship, he is the only true God. It is not true merely because Christ declared it to be true. It is true because adopting God's worldview is the only way human beings can properly function. **Surrendering our lives to Jesus is not a religious choice! It is medical choice that allows human beings to achieve a healthy psychological perspective and attitude towards themselves, their relationships and life, in general.**

When God is at the center of our lives, we gain God's perspective on life and adopt the proper psychological orientation towards our neighbor. Jesus summed up God's Law in these two statements: "Love the Lord your God with all your heart and with all your soul and with all your strength and with all your mind" and "Love your neighbor as yourself." (Luke 10:27, NIV) God created us to have deep and loving relationships. He was less interested in giving us creature comforts and more interested in developing His character in us, which made it more likely for us to experience the depth and meaning in our relationships that God has experienced with His triune partners from the beginning of time. Surrendering the authority of our lives to God is the only expression He accepts as loving Him with all of your heart, all of your strength, all of your soul, and mind. Only when we love Him more than we love ourselves and our lives, will we be able to experience the close, intimate relationships for which God created us. It is impossible to retain our self-centered nature and serve our fellow man the way God intended. Jesus wanted us to possess His servant's attitude. In Matthew 20:28 (NLT), He said, "For even the Son of Man came not to be served but to serve others and to give his life as a ransom for many."

God has known nothing but perfect relationships with each being of the divine trinity. The Father, who created us; Jesus, who lived with us; the Holy Spirit, who lives within His butterflies may have separate functions, but they all represent the same entity. Each one may play a different role in our lives, but they have always known that each member of their timeless relationship was valued equally. The triune God has lived in perfect community and relational harmony with Himself forever, and that is what He wants for his people, too.

After God created Adam, He said, "It is not good for man to be alone. I will make a helper suitable for him." (Gen. 2:18, NIV) So, He made Eve, who was different but equal and gave her as a companion to Adam. He wanted them to experience the joy of an intimate relationship with each other just as God had experienced within the Holy Trinity. Thus, God created a Marital Holy Trinity, man's most intimate relationship, designed to be three-sided between husband, wife and God. Husbands and wives were not expected to live their entire lives together without the guidance and assistance of God, because conflict is impossible to avoid when two sinners live in one house. Since the Trinity is one Spirit, He wants His married butterflies to become one flesh.

This Holy Union can only occur, when both spouses worship God; not themselves and not each other. They must see each other as having equal value in the eyes of God, so they can love the other as him or herself. He knows, once we are no longer pretending to be the god of our lives, we can finally treat our spouses equally because we consider their needs and interests to be equal to our own. Only then, can our marriages begin to reflect the harmonious image of our glorious triune God.

God is a relational being. In order for us to reflect His nature, we also must become fully relational human beings. In order for us to view our relationships as the most rewarding endeavor in life, we must be transformed in order to love people as ourselves. For this to happen, we must be told the absolute truth about ourselves, our purpose, and our world and only Jesus can do this. In fact, testifying to the truth was Christ's main mission while He was here on Earth. Yet, He not only testified to the truth, He was the Truth! Without entering a subservient relationship with Jesus, we will never know the truth about our lovability, our value to God and His desire for us to develop deeper and more intimate relationships.

So it is Jesus, not his message of truth that sets us free — free from the grinding and hopeless life of a caterpillar, who is condemned to spend his short time on Earth gorging on leaves and accumulating all the worldly stuff possible. No matter how many leaves a caterpillar consumes, he will never become full or satisfied. No matter how much wealth a caterpillar has accumulated, it will not guarantee that he will have rewarding relationships or be satisfied with himself and life, in general. In fact, his pride will insure this unhappy outcome.

In 1 Timothy 6:10 (NLT) it says, "For the love of money is the root of all kinds of evil. And some people, craving money have wandered from the true faith and pierced themselves with many sorrows." This is especially true in our culture today. God knew that if we continued to live as caterpillars, we would struggle to place developing relationships above pursuing wealth. Our selfish pursuits would ultimately result in lives marred by pathological and harmful interpersonal behavior that would cause us unnecessary pain and suffering. Our self-centered nature prevents our human relationships from becoming fully functional, joyful and rewarding. However, if we are willing to surrender to God and make Him our new master, we will truly be able to love and serve our neighbors, and our relationships will become much more fulfilling and meaningful. **Experiencing joyful relationships is easy when we serve God, and extraordinarily difficult when we serve ourselves.**

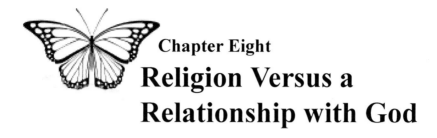

Chapter Eight
Religion Versus a Relationship with God

See to it that no one takes you captive by philosophy and empty deceit, according to human tradition, according to the elemental spirits of the world, and not according to Christ.

Colossians 2:8 ESV

"I wish it (Christianity) were more productive of good works ... I mean real good works ... not holy-day keeping, sermon-hearing ... or making long prayers, filled with flatteries and compliments despised by wise men, and much less capable of pleasing the Deity."

Benjamin Franklin

Man's understanding of God has varied over the millennia and has given rise to a multitude of religions worshipping numerous gods. However, ancient people had no real proof of God's existence or his true identity or identities. Nor had they any idea where they could find their gods or if they could be found at all. In order for these primitive caterpillars to feel like they had some control over their environment, they needed to assess the character of their individual god or gods so they could predict their behavior. They believed that they could behave in an acceptable way or perform certain rituals to earn their god's favor to escape his wrath, which they believed was behind the many natural disasters that befell them. As a result, caterpillar men constructed many sets of religious beliefs over the centuries that seemed reasonable depending upon their current understanding of nature. These ancient people had no divine message, such as the Bible, describing the character and personality of their god. They used their powers of deduction and compiled characteristics of their god to fit an image that made sense to them. Although caterpillar men were the weaker beings, their self-centered nature led them to believe they could actually devise ways to influence the mighty gods who controlled their world. The ancient caterpillars started by making offerings and sacrifices to their chosen gods. Then, they devised many rituals in an attempt to control or limit their god's judgment on their lives. Over time, as their religious practices became more elaborate, they cataloged their rituals and laws in written form.

Throughout history, our caterpillar ancestors have worshipped animals and idols. However, the belief that there was only one sovereign God in control of the universe and their individual lives began with the Jews, God's chosen people. Monotheism was born. The Jewish people worshipped a single Holy God and followed an extensive set of laws given to them by their God. Several millennia later, Jesus came to free the Jews from trying to earn their salvation by perfectly keeping the laws of their religion. He offered them, through his crucifixion and resurrection, eternal salvation and a direct relationship with God. Nearly seven centuries later, Mohammed also worshipped a single god, Allah. Mohammed compiled a variety of laws into the Koran, which governed individual and social behavior. He called his book the Koran and his religion, Islam. In my opinion, this was a regressive move from Christianity because his followers returned to worshipping the law, just like the Jews did before Christ.

Mohammed disregarded the Christian idea of having a direct relationship with God. This was problematic because without a relationship with God, Islamic caterpillars were condemned to remain caterpillars for the rest of their lives. As I said before, caterpillars and butterflies can not surrender their authority to a set of rules, rituals, and laws. They can only attempt to follow them. No matter how well caterpillars adhere to their religious laws, their conformity to the law can never serve as a substitute for having a relationship with God. Without a loving connection with God, they can never become butterflies. No matter how many virtuous deeds their individual religion may inspire, they will be inadequate to bribe God into their service, and will have no effect on God's character or His plans for His creation.

Practicing a religion will not allow God to transform caterpillars into butterflies because caterpillars can devote themselves to keeping religious laws, yet not know or love God. Without submitting their lives into His transforming hands, they can not participate in a loving relationship with God. They mistakenly believe that if they adequately obey their religious beliefs, laws, and rituals it will be possible to earn God's favor to do *their* will. This is the definition of a "salvation by works" religion. It is a barter system. If they do for Him, He will do for them. No love is required. Practicing a religion does nothing to change a caterpillar's self-centered perspective on life, because he is treating God just as he treats his fellow caterpillars. He is trying to manipulate God to provide for his needs and wants. **A salvation by works religion about God is ultimately designed to have God fulfill man's will. A relationship with God allows man to know and serve God's will.**

Since our perspective is unchanged, practicing a religion is still focused on fulfilling our desires, not God's. In addition to remaining the central figure in our lives, religious life still requires us to earn our significance by seeking another person's approval or affirmative opinion. The only difference is that we have changed our target audience from people to God. The religious caterpillar has moved from earning a person's approval to seeking God's approval in order to bolster his own sense of significance and control.

Caterpillars have used their substantial, yet limited, intellect to design religions, which are plans they believed would help them manipulate or bribe God into their service. On the surface, people who rigorously observe a set of religious laws and rituals may appear devoutly religious. However, as long as they have not submitted to the person of God, their efforts remain a vain attempt to gain greater influence and favor with God. **Throughout the ages, practicing a religion has allowed people to try to get right with God without having to relinquish living as their own god.**

Occasionally, practicing a religion makes caterpillars feel and behave humbly, but it fails to give them a humble and loving nature. In fact, some religions do the opposite by justifying the caterpillar's self-centered nature. This form of religion teaches that those who reject their beliefs are inferior or corrupt, rather than equal and lost. Islam is the most notable example of this type of religion. It is perfectly suited for caterpillars because its followers are encouraged to see the world from man's congenitally superior perspective. Islam does not believe their God transforms man's nature. It accepts the fact that man's nature is sinful (dysfunctional), so the only way to construct an orderly society is to restrict and control the behavior of its followers.

The Koran is consistent with this viewpoint. Mohammed included numerous laws that placed tight restrictions on personal and public behavior, which allowed him and future Islamic leaders to control their followers through fear of banishment, harsh punishment or death. Muslims do not believe Allah can change the evil nature of his own followers. The only thing Islam offers human beings is another system of punishments and rewards to keep people in line. Islam, like any other caterpillar religion, is about maintaining control over their caterpillar people by forcing them against their congenital evil nature to behave better. Mandatory obedience to religious law ensures control over believers, while obedience to God offers freedom to believers.

Islamic caterpillars, like all caterpillars, are self-centered. From their perspective, they believe and insist that Allah must be the true and supreme God. Therefore, their laws must be seen as superior to the laws of other religions and must be obeyed by all or violators will pay the heavy and sometimes painful consequences. Unbelievers, known as infidels, are not only thought to be wrong, Muslims consider infidels to be less valuable than their Muslim brethren. Since followers of the Islamic faith believe their religion is superior to all other religions, then people who practice other religions are considered to be inferior and are treated as such. In fact, members of minority religions who live within Islamic societies may have their religious activities restricted because the infidel's religious or cultural beliefs might tempt them away from their Islamic roots. Unlike a follower of Jesus, a Muslim can not undergo a transformation into a butterfly because his religion leaves him as self-centered and superior as any secular caterpillar.

Since Islam is a salvation by works religion, interfering with a Muslim's adherence to the law may compromise his ability to earn Allah's favor. This interference can not be tolerated for long because a caterpillar's god-like significance is dependent upon getting his own way. Islamic fundamentalists do not tolerate an infidel's opposing religious or political views. In the case of Jewish people, Muslims have dehumanized them to such a degree that they consider them no better than pigs or monkeys. If Muslims consider infidels a mere stumbling block on the road to a worldwide caliphate, then the lives of these dehumanized infidels will be considered expendable. The tenets of Islam compel their caterpillar followers to rise and fight against opposing political and cultural entities, and their belief in the superiority of Islam justifies killing those who refuse or rebel against the teachings of their prophet, Mohammed. Islam employs the evil within man's nature to eliminate those who they perceive to be opponents of their religious beliefs. Therefore, conversion to Islam by coercion, direct force or terrorism becomes acceptable.

I would like to take a moment to draw a sharp contrast between Islamic caterpillars and Christian butterflies. Christ-centered butterflies also seek to evangelize unbelievers, but the Christian way is completely contrary to Islamic conversion. This is because Christianity is not a religion like Islam. Salvation for a Christian is not about adherence to divine laws. It is a result of developing a relationship with Jesus. Therefore, Christians do not need to force their religious laws on others to establish or maintain their significance and control, because religious laws have nothing to do with earning their significance or salvation. Becoming a Christian requires a spiritual reconnection with God, so God, Himself, can transform people into His likeness, and send them the Holy Spirit to help them *internally control* their own behavior. **Since placing one's faith in Jesus is the only requirement for salvation, there is no further need to impose religious law on anyone. For this reason, there can never be a Christian theocracy.**

If the Muslim's nature remains self-centered, then the nature of Islamic society will also be self-centered and evil. This psychological perspective will eventually lead to internal and interpersonal conflict. This means that the Islamic worldview is incompatible with having inner psychological peace or a harmonious and peaceful world. **Believing that Islam is a religion of peace is an oxymoron because peace is incompatible with the concept of inequality of people. Peace can only occur when human beings consider all people equal under the law and in the eyes of God, i.e. Christianity.**

Muslims behave just like any other caterpillars. The lower their sense of self-worth, the more power they will wield against others to make themselves feel superior again. Therefore, when their failure to keep the law makes them feel guilty, ashamed or unworthy, and forgiveness is not assured, the acceptable way to assuage these feelings is to take action to earn Allah's favor by entering into jihad, a holy war against the infidels. Instead of hiding in the bushes like Adam, they hide behind the cloak of jihad to defend Mohammed's holy name and Allah's superiority. Hopefully, they can regain Allah's favor by impressing him with the vigor of their defense of Islamic law or any offense against Muhammad. Maybe he will be merciful and overlook their transgressions against His laws and allow them to be admitted to Paradise. Better yet, they can guarantee their admittance into Paradise by dying as martyrs.

We have seen this scenario manifested in the brutality of Shari'ah law as they commit their terrorist acts against their own people and other infidels. How many times have we heard Muslims defend Allah's supremacy by proclaiming, "God is great!" as they commit a murder or a beheading? It appears that they assault or kill their fellow man in the name of protecting the honor of their god or their prophet, Muhammad. When you think about it, the only people who promote Shari'ah law are those who think they will be enforcing it, not those who will be subject to it. This notion of defending the superiority of their God is quite nonsensical because if they truly believed Allah was an omnipotent god, he would not need to be defended. It seems illogical that the weaker mortals should sacrifice their lives to defend an all-powerful god. In the Christian faith, Jesus did not ask us to die to protect Him. He died to save us.

The Muslim way of earning Allah's favor can be easily perverted because they worship the laws in the Koran. Just like any religious person who worships the written law instead of participating a loving relationship with God, Muslim leaders can either ignore or emphasize any of the passages in the Koran that will serve their personal or political purposes. For example, the Koran is said to contain over a hundred "war verses" and fewer than ten "peace verses." Muslim leaders can choose to emphasize any verse that will incite their fellow Muslims to achieve their religious, political, military or criminal purposes. If they desire power or control, as caterpillars usually do, they can emphasize verses that will make their followers willing to martyr themselves in the act of killing others. In contrast, followers of Christ can also become martyrs, but since butterflies have a loving relationship with God, it will be in the act of steadfastly professing their faith in Christ in the face of their imminent death or in the selfless act of protecting and defending others. The Islamic act of martyrdom represents the purest form of evil towards one's neighbor, while the act of a Christian martyr represents the greatest love a man can exhibit.

Clearly, it is a human being's self-centered nature that is the source of all evil in the world! Unfortunately, the hallmark of salvation by works religions is that they seem to magnify and justify man's self-centered nature, rather than minimize or eliminate it. Only surrendering to God's will, in love, can transform man's congenital, self-centered nature. Practicing a religion about God will not do it. Even becoming a Christian will not change a man's nature if his Christian faith is merely practiced as a religion rather than a relationship with Jesus. We must live totally under His authority, like we were His slaves, in order to see the world from His perspective. We can never attain God's worldview unless we will stop thinking and acting as if we were the primary focus of our lives. The Old and New Testament lists many rules and commandments designed to improve our lives. However, until Christians make Christ their Lord, as well as their Savior, and make themselves His servants rather than living as if He is their servant, religious Christians will fail to adhere to God's Law even if they desire to do so.

Islam is the most notable of the salvation by works religions. However, the practice of any of these religions can never be pleasing to God. Hebrews 11:6 (NIV) corroborates this statement. It says, "and without faith, it is impossible to please God, because anyone who comes to him must believe that he exists and the he rewards those who earnestly seek him." This passage did not say anything about keeping religious law as a substitute for having faith in God. There is a paradox regarding the practice of any salvation by works religion. **Although these types of religions are designed to express faith in God through ritualistic worship, practicing these religions actually makes it impossible to place their total faith in God.** How can this be? When we practice a religion, our ability to earn God's favor is dependent upon *our* ability to follow the rules. Therefore, as we work to earn God's favor, we must place our faith in ourselves and *our* ability to keep the Law rather than in God's grace and generosity to provide for us and answer our prayers. The Bible clearly states that without faith in God, and God alone, He can never be pleased. Consequently, God can never be pleased with us when our primary method of worship is simply to follow religious law and tradition. To God, the strict worship of religious laws represents nothing more than another form of idolatry. Worshipping the Koran, the Talmud or even the Bible, for that matter, is an unacceptable substitute for having a direct, intimate and loving relationship with God.

How can people ever have true faith in God? They can only have faith in God if they do not have to earn whatever God offers, such as the gift of grace, forgiveness of sin and eternal salvation. Jesus is the only God who offers caterpillars these gifts. Grace is like an undelivered gift at the post office. It has already been paid for, and all the recipients need to do is decide to put their faith in Christ and pick it up. He does not require us to earn His favor. He freely showers His favor upon us. Therefore, people who submit their lives to Christ and follow Him have received their salvation without directly paying for their sins because Christ already paid that heavy price by dying on the cross. Placing our faith in Christ is different from practicing a religion because God's favor is no longer dependent upon us keeping the Law. In fact, there is nothing we can do to earn His favor or our eternal salvation. It is freely given to us once we accept Jesus as our true Lord and Savior.

Surrendering our lives to Christ is not a religious choice. It is a relational choice. It marks the beginning of a relationship that will allow us to develop a true faith in the provision and sovereignty of God. Developing a relationship with Jesus also allows a butterfly to live his life with a psychological advantage that is unavailable to caterpillars. In Hebrew 9:13-14 (NLT) it says, "Under the old system, the blood of goats and bulls and the ashes of a young cow could cleanse people's bodies from ceremonial impurity. Just think how much more the blood of Christ will purify our consciences from sinful deeds so that we can worship the living God." **Surrendering to Christ's authority allows human beings to experience total forgiveness and a clean conscience, free of guilt and shame. Through a relationship with Jesus, man's psyche, which is his personal judgment of himself, can be totally cleansed and**

renewed. After his rebirth, God considers a butterfly man clean and innocent, just the way Adam was prior to his fall from grace.

We, as born-again Christians, have become new creations, and unlike our first natural birth, the Spirit of God dwells within us from the first moment of our rebirth. This time we are fully aware that God is God, and we are not. We now have a new, more functional worldview regarding our future that will transform our nature and renew our lives. Surrendering our lives to God through Jesus marks the beginning of an intimate relationship with God, not the adoption of a Christian religion about God. As more people realize this, they will understand that Christianity represents the only psychologically healthy worldview. It is the Christian worldview, not the practice of the Catholic or Protestant religion that will help free people from the bondage of their self-serving nature. A new relationship with Christ will improve the mental health of all human beings living under His authority.

For Americans, whose country was founded and influenced by Judeo-Christian values, there are several meaningful benefits to correctly understanding that faith in Christ is not a religion. A relationship with God changes man's congenital worldview, and this worldview provides man with a healthier psychological perspective and understanding of life. **Since Christianity is not a religion, like Judaism and Islam, legal issues regarding separation of church and state should no longer exist.**

A second and equally important benefit from gaining the proper understanding of Christianity is that the Bible, which represents God's worldview, can be reclassified as a medical book; a psychological textbook rather than a religious one. The Biblical worldview, which proclaims that God is in control, is necessary to achieve optimal mental and relational health and should be taught, once again, in public schools throughout America. Adopting a perspective that helps human beings counter their evil nature will lead to healthier living and a more peaceful world. Surrendering to God through

Jesus is not a method for making man into a religious caterpillar. It is God's way of initiating the process of a man's transformation into a butterfly, who will become a more emotionally stable and content human being and a peaceful neighbor.

If the practice of religion falls short of truly loving God, then how much love and devotion do we need to offer Him to become acceptable to God? Jesus set the bar high for us when He said, "There is no greater love than to lay down one's life for one's friends." (John 15:13 NLT) Dying for his friends is exactly what Jesus did for us on the cross. God's greatest commandment has always been to love the Lord, God with all of your heart, mind and strength. This means we have to offer Him our maximum love. We have to love God more than we love ourselves, our wives, our children or anyone else. He sacrificed His life for something he loved more; His people. Therefore, He expects us to sacrifice something we love and value above all else: our autonomy for something we love more — Our God, Our Father in Heaven.

When we have made Lord Jesus our master, we are no longer practicing a religion, but are embracing a relationship with the Lord of Lords, King of Kings, Almighty God. **We can now love God for who He is rather than what He can do for us.** After we receive the gift of the Holy Spirit, God's Spirit, who lives within us, we can be permanently included in a relationship with the triune God, the Creator of the Universe. When God's Holy Spirit lives in us, we are now able to share in God's joy, which we know emanates from His intimate relationship with His triune partners. What can be more awesome than that? Can we ever have a greater connection with God than to have His Spirit live within us? God wants us to have an intimate relationship with Him because without it, His people would remain dysfunctional beings who drift through life without purpose and experience less rewarding and meaningful lives. God wants us to worship Him, and Him alone, because only within a subservient relationship will we be able to function as He designed.

God's plan was not for us to behave according to His commandments so we could become healthy. He wanted us to become healthy through our relationship with Him, so we could obey His commandments and extend peace and good will towards our neighbors.

Religion and the Jewish Caterpillar

Throughout Jewish history, the Hebrew people yearned for the coming of the promised Messiah. However, the Messiah did not deliver God's chosen caterpillars, the Jews, from their oppressors as they had envisioned. Instead, Jesus came to give them something more enduring. He came to save them from their sinful nature by offering Himself as their new and proper God. He came to heal all of His lost children, Jews and Gentiles alike, who had been scarred from centuries of suffering. God gave His "chosen people" the Ten Commandments and many other laws to help govern their society. These laws were certainly helpful and full of wisdom, but they were so specific and numerous, the Jewish caterpillar could never consistently obey them all. God wanted His people to understand through their experience with the Law that no matter how determined they were to be obedient, they would inevitably sin against Him. He was setting the stage for the coming Messiah. However, they needed more than a one-time hero to free them of Roman tyranny, they needed a Savior to forgive their sins and prepare them for eternity with God.

Without an intimate, loving relationship with God, they could only build a legalistic religion about Him. In spite of their sinful ways, God sent His Son among His chosen people, while they were still sinners, to sacrifice His life for them. He wanted to set His Jewish caterpillars free from the frustration of trying to perfectly keep His Law as a means of attaining salvation. God wanted their love, not just their obedience to the Law, as a measure of their devotion to Him. Having a loving relationship with His people is the main reason God created man.

God's Jewish people prayed to Him, but they worshipped their ancestors, traditions and the materialism of the world. In the New Testament Gospels, we read that Jesus discovered the Jewish caterpillar priests, who dedicated themselves to keeping the Law of Moses, had turned the temple into a market place for their own financial gain. Jesus rebuked them by accusing them of keeping the law to glorify themselves rather than God. Jesus knew that any set of laws, civil or religious, can be twisted, subverted, cherry-picked or totally ignored to suit the needs of those people in power. That is why He wanted them to worship Him, not the Law. Whereas the Law can be manipulated, God can not!

I doubt that God was surprised that the ultra-religious Pharisees could appear devoutly religious while continuing to live as their own god. Since they had not yet submitted their authority to Jesus, eventually they would succumb to their self-serving, evil nature. They would resort to behaving just like men who ignored the Law, and use their elevated religious status to exert power over the people they promised to serve. The Pharisees used their powerful positions to boost their own sense of significance, just like the most common caterpillars. These were Israel's most religious Jews, yet even God's most devoted followers could not keep from being corrupted by their sinful nature.

The Jewish Pharisees had no trouble accusing Jesus of blasphemy when He proclaimed Himself to be God. Unfortunately, they could not see that by worshipping the Law rather than God, they were committing idolatry, which also was blasphemous. They noticed the proverbial speck in the eye of their neighbor, but when it came to their own self-centered, god-like behavior, they could not see the plank in their own eye. **Caterpillars can not see that practicing salvation by works religions is self-serving and idolatrous, and can never represent faithful worship to God.**

God condemns our caterpillar desire to be our own god as blasphemy, which always excludes man from God's transforming power. Our persistence in choosing our ways above God's ways condemns us to remain unfinished, immature and dysfunctional larvae that will never be transformed to reflect the nature and likeness of their Father. **When God commanded us to love the Lord God with all of our hearts, minds, and strength, it was not merely so we would show God proper respect and reverence. It was a necessary step for His caterpillars to become butterflies and achieve their maximum psychological, emotional and spiritual health.**

The bottom line is that religion does not make us less evil and more loving human beings. When we practice a religion, our self-centered nature remains intact. We can only become fully functional when we resume the same relationship orientation with our Creator that existed before the Fall of Man; a relationship where God was in control and man was not. Since Adam and Eve never practiced a religion in the Garden of Eden, why would God expect us to practice one outside of the Garden?

Jesus, Religion and Satan's Lie

Jesus did not come to Earth to become the leader of a new religion. There is nothing in the Gospels to suggest that Jesus came to Earth to gather followers to start a new religious movement. He never even disavowed Himself as a Jew or proclaimed Himself the leader of a new earthly sect of Judaism. Although Jesus is an awesome teacher, He did not come to teach us how to behave like Him because He knew we could not suppress our evil nature long enough to consistently imitate His good and godly behavior. Jesus could not heal us by merely telling us what was wrong with us and showing us the proper way to behave. He knew the only true way to correct our sinful behavior was to give us a means of countering it. For this to occur, Christ had to redeem our lives by experiencing an excruciating death on the cross. He had to die so that our new nature, His nature, would come to life in us. Only then could we behave more like Jesus.

Jesus did not ransom His life for mankind, so people could remain Jews, Muslims, Buddhists, or Hindus. Nor was His desire to make us into Methodists, Baptists, Catholics, Episcopalians or any other Christian denomination. He died in order to rescue us from the selfish, dysfunctional life of a caterpillar and make us into butterflies. God never wanted us to replace a relationship with Him with a religion about Him. He knew that the establishment of multiple religious sects would cause each group to compete for his favor and further separate His people. Man's development of religion was a self-centered act designed to compete for God's approval, as if God could be bribed into serving the winners.

God is the Creator of the Universe; the entire cosmos and the living beings who occupy it. The prefix "uni" means one, single or whole. God designed his Creation to be unified and connected. Diversity of personalities, talents, races and languages is God's gift to His people because it takes all types of people to make the body of Christ appealing and functional. However, unity is God's call. This is reflected in America's motto, "E Pluribus Unum" (out of many, one). God's desire was to transform all of His self-centered caterpillars into God-centered butterflies, who possessed one nature and worshiped only one God. Butterflies may appear in a variety of colors and sizes, but they have all been remade to see the world from God's singular perspective. Diversity of people may make the world appear more interesting and unique, but worshipping a diverse number of gods and practicing different religions makes living much more dysfunctional and perilous.

Practicing different religions or developing Christian denominations is contrary to God's desire for us because attending a Baptist or Methodist church, in itself, does not transform us into butterflies. It just sets religious caterpillars apart into separate and less cohesive groups. The relationships between caterpillar denominations, just like relationships between individual human beings, are often more like competitions than partnerships. Since religions can never transform us into butterflies, God will not be satisfied with caterpillar's ritualistic display of worship. If caterpillars refuse to live under His authority, they interfere with His Will, and regardless how many knees religious caterpillars bend before God, they will never please Him.

Living under God's authority as a butterfly has a much greater impact on our lives than being a caterpillar trying to adhere to a set of religious rules and laws. God knows we would be more obedient to His Commandments if we followed them out of deep love for Him rather than out of obligation to Him. The same is true with human beings. Do we think our children would follow our rules better if they felt compelled to do so out of fear of punishment? Or, would they would be more obedient if they submitted to our authority out of a deep love for us? The answer should be obvious.

God conceived His plan to reconnect with His people before Adam and Eve were residing in the Garden of Eden. Jesus was to die on the cross so He could rescue His caterpillars from the legalism of Judaism, and set them free from being a slave to their self-centered nature. In Max Lucado's book, *Just like Jesus*, he wrote, "God loves you just the way you are, but he refuses to leave you that way." Mr. Lucado understood that one can not have a personal encounter with Jesus and remain unchanged. God created caterpillars perfectly, but He knew they would be too self-centered to relate to Him and others in a truly loving and meaningful way. God loved us so much He was willing to die, so it would be possible for us to complete our transformation into butterflies. He wanted us to have a loving relationship with Him and gain a new lease on life.

If God's original plan was to have a mutually loving *relationship* with us, then practicing a loveless *religion* was never God's desire for his people. Just as, the larval caterpillar was never meant to be the final form of God's insect creation, the lukewarm, legalism of the Jewish religion was never our Heavenly Father's ultimate plan for His chosen caterpillars. Since there are only two spiritual forces in the world, God and Satan, and religion was never God's plan, religion could only have been devised and instigated by Satan, the ruler of this world. **Satan's plan to keep caterpillars separated from God was ingenious. If he could deceive caterpillars into believing that practicing a religion was sufficient to make them right with God, He could prevent them from seeking a loving relationship with God that would reconnect them to Him!** The reason we humans are so easily deceived is because Satan's Lie regarding religion is so enormous. It completely fills our visual field and totally obstructs our view of God's truth. Religion blinds us from seeing that anything short of dying unto ourselves is truly self-worship or idolatry.

In addition to keeping human beings separated from God, practicing a religion tends to drive us emotionally further from Him. Again this is paradoxical. Since no human being can perfectly obey every law and observe every tradition all the time, people tend to experience more guilt and shame with each failure. These negative emotions result in feelings of inadequacy, which are universal to all who sincerely practice religions. The accumulative effect of their guilt and shame lowers their individual esteem, which may cause them to hide from God just like Adam and Eve did after they disobeyed Him and ate the forbidden fruit. When people feel like they have disappointed God or their prayers go unanswered, they may interpret their unfulfilled requests as their failure to earn His favor. This leads to a sense of inadequacy, which may leave them feeling unsure about their value to God. **Trying to keep all the laws of any religion, which is virtually impossible for anyone to do, will most likely keep people mentally and emotionally separated from God.** This is exactly the opposite effect man's religions were intended to have on us. Satan is so sly.

The practice of religion keeps caterpillars wingless and earth-bound. If caterpillars could see through the devil's plan and enter into a relationship with God, they would be transformed into butterflies with wings to overcome the world's gravitational force that is continuously trying to pull them away from their Heavenly Father. Jesus transformed His wayward caterpillars' self-centered nature into the God-centered nature of a butterfly by replacing their religion about God with a direct relationship with God. Jesus became the way for God's pedestrian caterpillars to acquire the wings to fly over Satan's devilishly constructed ravines, which throughout the millennia, kept billions of lost and wandering caterpillars separated from God. Since Jesus is the only way to reconnect us to our Creator, we have to confess our sins and profess our faith in Him, so God could finish our transformation. Christ's victory over Satan is complete since He thwarted Satan's mission to keep us caterpillars from a loving and transforming relationship with God. Man's acceptance of Christ's death on the cross makes it possible for us to have a right relationship with God. It is obvious to all born-again butterflies that no matter how well they may have practiced their previous religion as caterpillars, religion could never have reconciled them with their Creator.

Since love can only occur within a relationship, and true worship can only happen when we love God, then it takes a direct, personal relationship with God for us to develop a deep love for Him. Since organized religion can be practiced without loving God or submitting to His authority, religion is merely a way of giving lip service to God. It is a form of self-glorification we hope will make us feel more important or superior, so we do not see ourselves as just another insignificant group of caterpillars. Since the true focus of religion is still on man, not God, then religion is nothing more than a ruse that caterpillars hope will fool God into serving them. Frankly, it is the epitome of pride and arrogance to think that this scheme might work. Such is the nature of the unsaved caterpillar. **Ah, vanity! This is truly one of Satan's favorite sins.**

Chapter Nine
Political Worldview: The Primacy of Man or Law

But, now apart from the law the righteousness of God has been made known, to which the Law and the Prophets testify. This righteousness is given through faith in Jesus Christ to all who believe...

Romans 3:21-22 NIV

"If we ever forget that we are One Nation under God, then we will be a Nation gone under."

Ronald Reagan

Previously, I have shown that human nature changes depending upon whether we live under our own authority or under God's authority. Man is born to see himself as the god of his life, so he lives as if he is the primary person in his world. This results in a self-centered perspective and worldview, which is the source of the natural man's self-centered nature. Our worldview determines our psychology, which directs the manner in which we interact with others and live our lives. **This axiom also holds true in the development of our personal politics. Self-centered people are drawn to a form of government that satisfies man's worldview, and God-centered people are drawn to a form of government that is consistent with God's worldview.**

I believe the psychology of the caterpillar's political nature develops in the following manner: A self-centered caterpillar naturally believes in the primacy of man, which means he places his own importance above God. Just as the caterpillar wants to run his own life, he also wants to run his own government and will choose to follow his own man-made laws over God's Laws and scriptural wisdom. Caterpillar governments ignore God and will inevitably worship their legal system while butterfly governments honor God by acknowledging His authority in their society and political system.

Sadly, since our untransformed caterpillar citizens place their faith in man's laws rather than in God's authority, they will end up pursuing legalism in government just as they did in their religion, and they will elevate keeping the law above serving the well-being of their citizen. As I previously quoted from Matt. 6:24 (NIV), "No one can serve two masters. They will be devoted to the first, and despise the second." Caterpillar citizens who serve the law will despise God and discount the rest of those for whom Christ died.

Man was created to worship God, not the law. He was merely to obey the law so that society would be more civil. Having an orderly society is an admirable goal, but it is no substitute for a holy, God-centered society that exists to preserve the liberty of its citizens. Caterpillar governments use laws and regulations to control man's behavior in order to create their orderly society, i.e. Islam, Communism, Socialism. Their laws must be extremely intrusive, even oppressive, in order to force their fellow caterpillars to behave contrary to their selfish nature and submit to governmental authority. **Caterpillar people require a big, intrusive religious or secular government because they worship a small god; themselves and their laws.**

Butterfly governments operate in the opposite way. Rather than using restrictive laws to control the evil-nature of self-centered citizens, butterflies want a society in which Christ transforms the evil nature of its citizens, so they desire to obey His laws and the laws of the land. Since butterflies already worship God, they do not need government to become their God. Therefore, government is to be limited because it is man-made, and unlike God, it can never be all things to all people. **Butterflies desire a small government because they worship a big God.**

Contrary to the sacrificial behavior of Jesus, who freely paid the price for our freedom by rescuing us from slavery to sin, government always wants something in return for its generosity and entitlements. Butterflies know that every time a government offers something to its citizens, it will cost those citizens some of their freedoms. From a butterfly's perspective, worshipping government would not only be counter productive, it would be pure foolishness. Jesus died to set us free; free from man's evil nature. Butterflies know that caterpillar governments are incapable of consistently maintaining the best interest of its citizens at heart, and will eventually seek enough control to dominate them.

God wants His people to respect and obey the law, not out of fear or obligation, but out of love and respect for Him. He wants them to love their neighbors as themselves without needing to be constrained or directed by a system of laws. As disciples of Christ, man will follow His example of love and service. Jesus professed this truth in John 13:35 (NIV), "By this all men will know you are my disciples, if you love one another."

When Jesus healed the sick on the Sabbath, He demonstrated that loving people was to be placed above obedience to the law. The law must never be valued above the well-being and lives of our neighbors. I am not suggesting that butterflies made in God's image should ignore our laws, for observing the law is beneficial to every person and is necessary for a moral and stable society. However, when the well-being or the actual lives of our neighbors are in peril, obedience to civil law should become secondary. For example, recently a man's home caught fire. When the fire department arrived, they realized this man had not paid the seventy-five dollars for fire protection. The homeowner offered payment immediately on site, but the fire fighters adhered to the law and refused to put out the fire. How legally righteous would the county government have looked in court if someone had died in the fire? A government with a butterfly worldview would have put out the fire and dealt with the noncompliant man at a later date.

The proper context in which we are to view the law is consistent with the words of Jesus when he proclaimed, **"The Sabbath was made for man, not man for the Sabbath."** Mark 2:27, (NIV). The Sabbath was the Jewish people's most observed law to which they were universally devoted. On this day, no work was to be done, with few exceptions, such as delivering a baby. The caterpillar Pharisees were so devoted to this Holy day, they occasionally put the Sabbath ahead of God's mandate to love and serve His people. They were to keep the Sabbath holy in remembrance of God's goodness. Yet, how godly could they be if they withheld their good deeds to those desperately in need on that holy day? A caterpillar's need for significance compels him to present a favorable image to others, so he will attempt to religiously adhere to civil laws because his allegiance is to the law, not to the people these laws are supposed to serve. Like the Pharisees, liberal caterpillars will choose to revere and worship the Law. **Butterflies believe the law was to serve man. Man was not to serve the law at the expense of his neighbors.**

It is worth repeating that, as God-centered people, butterflies no longer are psychologically driven to earn the favor and good opinion of their fellow man. They may want to do so, but they are not emotionally compelled to do so in order to prove their worth. Because God has determined their worth for all time, they tend to act in ways that are righteous before God, not man. God has declared a butterfly's value to be equal to His own. Therefore, out of love and gratitude, a butterfly seeks to please God by doing His will. Butterflies still honor the Sabbath, but now the Sabbath is Jesus, Himself. Since Jesus now lives within each butterfly, they find rest in Christ and observe the Sabbath seven days a week.

As a result of their transformation, butterflies accept the fact that they will live under God's authority. They would rather seek His righteousness than their neighbor's approval, which could be withdrawn at any time. Butterfly men have been given the character of God via the transforming work of Jesus. Therefore, serving their neighbors, not devotion to the law is the measure of man's fruitfulness in the eyes of God. **For God-centered men, character is everything, so effectively serving his neighbor is of paramount importance.**

People who have a caterpillar's psychological understanding of the world, believe that they live under man's authority, not God's. This creates a paradox for them from which they can not escape. As the primary person in their lives, they are the directors and controllers of their decisions and behavior. Yet, their significance is totally dependent upon presenting as perfect an image as possible, which means they need to *appear* to be obedient to all of man's laws. Because of their worldview, caterpillars find themselves in a quandary. Although they perceive man's laws to be supremely important, they will not be able to consistently obey them because obedience to any authority other than their own is contrary to their nature. If they feel their significance is decreasing or threatened, they will eventually violate the law and their individual value system. **Therefore, caterpillars tend to use their legs to bypass the law when it benefits them, or they use the law to trample their neighbor's rights when it serves their purpose.** Ultimately, their nature prevents them from obeying man's laws, just as it makes them incapable of perfectly obeying God's commandments.

The Liberal Caterpillar Worldview

Caterpillars, being self-centered and self-reliant, do not acknowledge the sovereignty of God or that He is the bestower of mankind's needs. Instead, they look to government, the pinnacle of man's intellect and power to be their provider, their judge, and the object of their worship. These people are called Humanists, Secular Progressives, or Liberals. Like every group of caterpillars who serve as their own god, their goal is to control mankind by creating a system of government to administer man-made laws reflecting their ideals.

A Humanist is a person deeply concerned about human values and dignity. They espouse reason, ethics and judgement while rejecting any religious basis for morality. A Secular Progressive similarly advocates for reform of social and moral issues that inevitably abolish God. They believe there is no inherit value in tradition, and they maintain that customs and morality should be revised from time to time as the social views of society change. A Liberal is similar to a Progressive except he focuses on correcting economic inequality, but also promotes a progressive government. The common denominator among these groups is that they exclude or denounce the role of God in people's lives. In other words, a butterfly can never be a Liberal, Humanist or Secular Progressive.

Progressives and Liberals are advocates for the caterpillar culture as they work to alter social mores and civic mandates that ensure their agendas based upon a godless prospective of humanity. These caterpillars will legislate and establish the government's laws assuming they are the supreme ruler who knows best for all. In essence, they are behaving as God. But unlike our Heavenly God, who created mankind and instituted laws based upon his omniscient holy judgement, the caterpillars create laws based upon their self-centered need to control mankind.

Caterpillars worship the created, not the Creator, so the laws they create will become the object of their worship. When liberal caterpillars put the worship of man's laws above worshipping the true God, which is exactly what I described in the previous chapter, they are essentially practicing a religion. **Therefore, Secular Progressivism and Liberalism are actually forms of religion.** As religions, Humanism, Secular Progressivism and Liberalism act as a force against God and His desire to have a relationship with man. Have you noticed that Secular Progressives and Liberals, not Conservatives, are removing crosses and nativity scenes from public view and are violating God's Natural Law by promoting homosexual marriage and abortion? These caterpillars truly believe that man was to live under the authority of man's laws, not the authority of God's morality and commandments.

Liberals, like the Pharisees of old, also want to be seen as moral and compassionate people. Unfortunately, liberal morality is man-made, not God-given, which means each caterpillar person can ignore God's moral code and construct his own morality. For example, consider the concept of personal responsibility. God's entire plan for our *eternal* salvation depends on personal responsibility. He holds each of us accountable for accepting or rejecting His Son. No other person or group of people can make that decision for us. Unless a caterpillar personally places his faith in Christ and is born-again as a butterfly, he will not see heaven. Jesus reaffirms this point when He proclaims in John 3:3 (NIV), "I tell you the truth, no one can see the kingdom of God unless he is born again."

God's moral position regarding man's primary *earthly* responsibility is clearly expressed in the second half of 2 Thessalonians 3:10 (NIV). It says "If a man shall not work, he shall not eat." God puts the moral responsibility on the individual to earn his keep, not society or government to provide for him. God knows that when people persevere in their struggle to make ends meet and fulfill their responsibility to provide for themselves and their families, they develop personal integrity and character, which improves their self-worth. However, if people are truly incapable of working or are diligently working, but can not support themselves, they are not discarded and thrown to the wolves. God's mandate for individual responsibility is always tempered with His grace and mercy. God first expects people to be personally responsible, but if necessary, He will extend His grace to them by ministering to them personally or through His butterflies that will give generously to them. It has been America's Christian nature that has made us the most generous society the world has ever known.

Liberal morality, on the other hand, dictates that government should be compassionate to those not working by giving them nearly endless unemployment compensation or welfare. Their version of morality focuses first on being merciful, and it relegates personal responsibility to a distant second. If mercy, which is not making people pay the consequences of their irresponsible behavior, or grace, which is giving them something good they do not deserve, precedes personal responsibility, people will less likely become personally responsible.

This philosophical reversal of God's Biblical treatment of human beings will inevitably cause social dysfunction and government's financial collapse. Consider this simple illustration to explain the difference between a caterpillar and a butterfly's understanding of the moral and psychologically healthy treatment of people. When butterflies offer to help their neighbor by putting gas in his car, they first require him to remove his car's gas cap before they fill the tank. When caterpillars offer to fill their neighbor's tank, they pump the gas without ever requiring the recipient to do something as little as removing his gas cap. It is obvious that this philosophical reversal of God's morality has driven Liberals to pump trillions of dollars down the drain in the name of compassion. Sadly, the poor still have no gas in their tanks, which leaves them unable to drive away from the public trough and resume independent lives.

Caterpillar liberals are not stupid. They are just self-centered. Liberal caterpillars are psychologically driven to appear compassionate and powerful. They want those who directly receive government assistance to be beholden to them so that they can insure the allegiance of these voters. Like any typical caterpillar, these liberal politicians dole out entitlements with the ultimate goal of controlling the dependent population. Psychologically, liberals want to be viewed as the people's savior, because this fits their god-like perception of themselves.

Their worldview is counter-productive because it does not promote personal responsibility, which blunts the maturation and character of those who receive their neighbor's hard-earned money. People with less character and integrity will create a less functional, productive and harmonious society. **Butterflies are concerned with developing their fellow man's character. Liberal caterpillars are primarily**

concerned with maintaining their own compassionate image.

Caterpillar Liberals believe maintaining control makes them stronger, which reinforces their sense of significance. Unfortunately, it also increases their natural propensity for evil. In Matthew 23:27-28 (NLT) Jesus said, "What sorrow awaits you teachers of religious law and you Pharisees. Hypocrites! For you are like whitewashed tombs-beautiful on the outside but filled on the inside with dead people's bones and all sorts of impurity. Outwardly you look like righteous people, but inwardly your hearts are filled with hypocrisy and lawlessness." God's chosen people outwardly prayed to God, but they worshipped the Law and ancient Jewish traditions. Their society truly operated under the Pharisee's authority because most had no loving relationship with God. Without that relationship, they could not get to know God well enough to submit to living under His authority. Like the Jewish caterpillars of old, our current day liberal caterpillars hold the same self-centered worldview, which makes them rebel against living under anyone's authority except their own. The fact that Judaism is a religion rather than a relationship with God may explain why so many of my Jewish brothers and sisters appear so comfortable following the religion of Liberalism.

In order for Liberals to maintain their sense of superiority, they must feel powerful, and power is measured by how much control they have over others. Practically speaking, the self-image of a liberal or secular progressive politician is dependent upon winning conflicts and passing legislation by any means necessary. This liberal trait becomes most evident during debates when they are attempting to defend their positions. If they can not win on the merits of their case, they will resort to smearing or berating their opponents in order to make themselves *feel* superior to their opponents and *appear* superior to their constituents. This is the doctrine of personal destruction. They are psychologically compelled to maintain their superior image even if they must personally attack and destroy their opponents.

Although trying to control other people's opinions is a never-ending job, caterpillars are internally driven, like slaves, to persevere in this impossible task because preserving their god-like image depends upon it. Unfortunately for them, life is counterintuitive to man's way of thinking. **The more man tries to become the lord of his life, the more he needs to control others to maintain his sense of primacy. The more significant he needs to feel, the more he becomes a slave to the opinion of the very people he is trying to defeat or control.** The caterpillar politician may win the battle, but he will never win the war because there will always be that next voter or colleague he must impress to reinforce his sense of significance.

The Conservative Worldview

Conservatives are either God-centered butterfly people that are secure in the knowledge that God is in control of their lives and our country, or God-oriented caterpillars that believe that there is an entity out there greater than themselves, but have not submitted themselves to Christ to be transformed into butterflies. In fact, many of these caterpillars may or may not identify themselves as a member of a religion at all. Butterfly conservatives revere and admire God, so they value godly character traits and personal integrity, which represent the likeness of Jesus. Conservative caterpillars also value honesty and personal responsibility, and they have a sense that there is a benefit to having a purpose in life other than serving themselves. I call this faction of conservatives *traditional* Americans. They may not realize that America's founding principles were Christian principles, but they believe in the principles written in our Constitution by our founding fathers. They value personal responsibility. However, they may not link it to the values promoted in the Bible. It is clear that not all conservative people who desire a small government are butterflies. However, in order to ensure that enough of our population returns to our founders' Biblical worldview, more caterpillars will need to be transformed into butterflies.

Libertarians also have a conservative ideology, but they want a small government for different reasons than butterflies. Libertarians desire a small government, but they do not want God's influence in government at all. They believe government should not interfere with a citizen's personal choices and behavior, nor do they want a governmental morality to be able to dictate society's moral choices. For example, they are willing to decriminalize or legalize some drug use, prostitution, gay marriage and other non-Judeo-Christian moral behaviors as long as they believe these behaviors will not directly or negatively affect them or other members of society. It is almost as if they promote small, unobtrusive government because they are not concerned with the detrimental and destructive effects a Godless morality has on their fellow man. Some Libertarians identify themselves as religious Christians and others claim no religion at all, but neither are butterflies that possess God's worldview. These will be my only comments regarding Libertarians, and I will exclude them as examples in my discussion of Conservatism.

Conservative butterflies, unlike liberal caterpillars, want to use their wings to lift up and empower others, not gain economic or political power, so they could use their many legs to walk all over them. I am sure you have heard the saying, "Don't just give a man a fish. Teach him to fish and he will have food every day of his life." Conservative butterflies know that justice not only involves teaching a man to fish. It also includes giving him an equal opportunity to fish. God does not want His butterflies merely to give a man a hand-out. He wants them to give him a hand up, just as God extended His hand of forgiveness to lift man out of his slavery to self-worship and sin. Butterflies know that giving a man the opportunity to provide for himself allows him to escape his slave-like dependence upon a cold, faceless government bureaucracy. Encouraging people to become more personally responsible will, over time, create an electorate that will desire small, limited government because they will not need a large, over-reaching government to subsidize them.

Butterflies, made in the likeness of Christ, are confident people because they have placed their hope in God, not in themselves and not in government, as do caterpillars. People who find hope in God feel more secure and security instills confidence. Confident people do not always need to be in control of every situation, for they ultimately know God is in control. Butterflies want to do God's will, so they work to free their fellow man from oppression. This is exactly what Christ did for us when He set us free from being slaves to our self-centered nature. Butterflies desire a small government because they know that if government becomes too powerful, it may become tyrannical and begin removing the unalienable rights God has endowed them.

A butterfly citizen desires to serve others, whereas, even the caterpillar with the best of intentions will inevitably betray his neighbors and resort to serving himself in order to preserve his sense of power and control. This is the most common complaint I have heard regarding our political, public servants. The passage of Obama's Health Care legislation is a case in point. It illustrated that many of our elected caterpillar officials will honor the will of their constituents as long as it does not interfere with their own personal will and political agenda. Because of their self-centered worldview and selfish nature, it would be foolish to believe that they could consistently put the nation's needs above their own.

If we want to ensure that our elected officials will, more often than not, put our country ahead of their political careers, we need to have butterflies serving in Congress and the Presidency. John Jay, the first Supreme Court Justice, affirmed my assertion in this statement he made over two centuries ago. He said, "Providence has given to our people the choice of their rulers, and it is the duty as well as the privilege and interest of our Christian Nation to select and prefer Christians for their rulers." Followers of Christ have a selfless nature, and will less likely abuse their positions of power to rule against the will of the people. Butterflies serve their neighbors. Caterpillars, ultimately, serve themselves. Conservatives tend to have a Biblical worldview and serve their neighbors. Liberals have a self-centered worldview and tend to serve themselves. Therefore, Conservatism leads to a more functional country. Liberalism does not.

The Failure of Fairness

Liberal people and politicians hold the same worldview as self-centered caterpillars. Therefore, they derive their significance from being liked by others. The easiest way to be liked is to be seen as fair-minded. This psychological perspective compels caterpillars to choose and follow the doctrine of *fairness*. Liberals may claim that they stand for "social justice," but they really mean "social fairness." Therefore, it is predictable that Liberals, Secular Progressives and Humanist's will promote legislation designed to achieve fairness in society. They will also design their foreign policy to convince other countries to see us as fair-minded people in an effort to make them like us. Unfortunately, fairness was not our founders' goal for America. It was "justice for all," which is consistent with God's character. God promises us just treatment, not fair treatment. **People who seek fairness want to be liked. People who insist on justice want to be respected.** People who believe in God and Biblical principles will naturally desire justice for their friends and neighbors. **As we all know, life is not fair! How foolish it is to try to develop a governmental philosophy that is contrary to this truth!**

If people respect us, and we are firm and consistent in our dealings with them, they will learn to trust us, even if our policies are not necessarily consistent with their own. People transformed into the likeness of God want to engender trust, for out of trust comes faith, and from faith comes hope. Practically speaking, people who trust us will be less likely to rise against us. If the people of the world only *like* us, they will rarely trust us because likability does not engender trust. Respect does. Whether or not foreigners decide to befriend us is a function of their individual and societal perspectives and their current leader's policies. Our behavior plays some role in the development of their opinion of us, but it will not override a foreigner's traditional antithetical worldview or generational hatred.

The notion that we can control other people's opinion of us is the primary miscalculation that emanates from a self-centered worldview; that people can control the thoughts, opinions and behavior of others. This is utterly untrue! The only way for other people to change their opinion of us is for their perspective and worldview to change. Being friendly to people, whose personal and historical worldview compels them to see us as enemies, aggressors or manipulators, will never develop trust in us regardless of our good deeds. If they do not trust us before we do our good deeds, our good deeds will be interpreted as manipulation or part of a plan to deceive them, and they will not *like* us or *trust* us.

For example, assume that we are trying to change Iran's opinion of us by giving them a year's supply of free food in an attempt to make them like us. Will they suddenly consider us friends, and trust us when we reassure them that we will not interfere with their pursuit of a nuclear bomb? Of course, not! Having a foreign policy designed to make them *like* us will always fail as long as Iranian society's current perspective and worldview remains the same.

Just like any human beings, the only way Iran's worldview will change is if Iranians come under control of a new authority. This new authority can be established either through an internal revolution or an American conquest. The former would be better than the latter because governing them as victors would only harden their hearts and reinforce their negative opinion of us. However, the optimal way to transform the Iranians perspective and worldview is for them to choose to live under Christ's authority rather than the Koran. Only then, could they see us as equals and believe that Americans are their friends. In fact, we would be better than friends. We would be seen as brothers and sisters in Christ.

As impossible as it seems, the next logical step required to change their worldview is to evangelize them. The loss of American lives will be massive whether we fight a war with them or send missionary after missionary to Iran, like lambs to the slaughter. Many of God's butterfly children will die introducing Jesus before the Iranian people believe our motivation is to spread God's love to them rather than to impose a new religion or political regime on them. Whether we like it or not, this is the process God uses to make disciples of all nations. Many times throughout history, Christian missionaries served and died long before the people to whom they ministered came to Christ. Jesus had to die on the cross before the disciples realized how much He loved them and came to full faith in Jesus for their salvation. With the exception of John, all of the Apostles died violently as a result of spreading the Good News of God to the world.

In the case of the Iranians or any other non-Christian country, it would be ideal if they would peacefully accept the Gospel and spiritually die unto themselves. However, this is unlikely to occur, for when it comes to human behavior, there can be no change without confrontation, and no confrontation without the possibility of conflict. This statement is true whether we are talking about a mental struggle within an individual's mind or a confrontation between two people or two entire nations.

Therefore, offering someone a new life involves some level of sacrifice on the part of both the evangelist and the evangelized. The evangelist may risk his *mortal life* to spread the Gospel, while the convert must lose his *autonomous life* to accept the Gospel. The result of Christian martyrdom in the act of spreading the Gospel, is not that the saved person will inevitably *like* the messengers. It is that the new Christian will ultimately *respect* them and those who preceded them. It is the missionary's sacrificial devotion to rescuing the lost from their dysfunctional lives and religion that will cause the Iranian people to trust them and the promise of the Gospel. Just as the Apostles would never allow themselves to be executed and crucified in the defense of a lie, those to whom we spread the Gospel will also know that Christian missionaries are not going to risk sacrificing their lives for what they believe is a lie, either!

As we would expect, those with a God-oriented conservative or

God-centered butterfly worldview are psychologically driven to choose the doctrine of justice, not fairness. Butterflies respect and revere God because He is just, not because He is fair. He will give us what we need, not what we want or think we deserve. Whether we merely believe in His existence or have already submitted our lives to Him, we will not be treated fairly by God because fairness is an assessment that is exclusively determined by humans. It is made based on our self-centered assessment of our own worth and man's erroneous understanding of the world. Judgment is determined by God, and while His judgment is always righteous, it is rarely equal. From the liberal caterpillar's perspective, if a policy does not lead to equanimity among people, it will not be fair. Since each of us has different spiritual and psychological needs, God does not treat all of us the same. For God to treat all people in the same manner would be similar to a doctor offering the same treatment to every patient regardless of his condition.

God deals with us based on our level and type of dysfunction (sin). He always acts in our best interest, yet we rarely consider it fair. Certainly God loves us, but He must judge our sin because meting out justice is ingrained in His nature. God will not alter His judgment because we belong to a certain religious group. In fact, the opposite is true. Practicing a religion involves following rituals and ancient traditions rather than having a loving relationship with God. Religion is nothing more than a form of idolatry that represents one more sin He must judge. God can not be bribed by our religious practices to abandon His perfect justice. Fortunately, for all people who merely practice religion, He has mercy and plenty of it.

Since God has made butterflies in His image, He knows His butterflies will also seek justice. When people are treated justly by others, they know that they have earned their accolades or their rebukes and punishments. When groups of people are treated fairly rather than justly, they are rewarded or punished in order to achieve parity between groups, not because they deserved it. The doctrine of fairness forces us to ignore or discount the role each group's behavior may have played in determining their circumstances. If God's people are never required to pay the consequences of their behavior, they will never look at themselves truthfully, and they will learn little that might improve their lives. We may be inspired on the mountain tops, but we develop character when we are in the valleys of our lives. When we prevent people from suffering the consequences of their behavior, we are tacitly condoning their behavior and are stunting their character development and proper understanding of life.

Politically Correct Speech

Another major problem with people who value fairness rather than justice is that they will play whatever word games are necessary to become politically correct. They need to be liked so much, they can not be honest in their description of other people's shortcomings or differences. For example, they may call a mentally retarded or disabled person "physically challenged" rather than "handicapped." These liberal, non-God-centered people are concerned about not offending the handicapped in hopes that handicapped and others in society will have a favorable opinion of them. Renaming the handicapped may make liberals feel less judgmental and more likable, but it does not change the handicapped person's reality. What the handicapped person wants is not a name change, but love, honesty and real accommodations to make his life better.

Liberal caterpillars are playing mind games with themselves. They do not want to acknowledge that the handicapped person is different from themselves. They might judge that person even less valuable to society than they do already. By renaming the handicapped person, the caterpillar is subconsciously trying to lessen his own guilt regarding his natural assessment that the handicapped person is inferior and less valuable to society.

Without a personal relationship with God, a caterpillar's erroneous understanding of what it means to be god is that they are superior, and others are, by definition, inferior and less important. This is not the case with our true God. Although He is sovereign over man, He does not see man as less valuable than Himself. In fact, He values man equal to Himself. Remember, Jesus came to redeem us with His own life. He sacrificed His life to offer eternal life to all of His neighbors, including the handicapped. Therefore, God does not have to rename man in order to assuage His guilt that would result from a superiority complex, because God has no guilt. He sees his creatures as having equal value to Himself. He does not try to make us *like* Him by calling those of us who occasionally disobey Him, "misguided." He calls us what we truly are, "sinners."

With regard to the handicapped, Christ-centered butterflies can see the handicapped as different from themselves, yet love them because they measure the impaired person's worth from God's perspective; all are equal in His eyes. Butterflies can be compassionate out of love for the handicapped, whereas caterpillars tend to be motivated out of pity for them, for they do not see them or anyone else as their equal. To be totally honest, God sees even His healthy caterpillars as handicapped because they are living without His spirit inside them. Without the indwelling of the Holy Spirit, all caterpillars have something missing inside them, and this deficiency will cause them to become dysfunctional. They are just like handicapped people, who have something missing inside that causes them to malfunction. The caterpillar's abnormal behavior may be less obvious than the mentally or physically handicapped person, but they are also dysfunctional human beings. In fact, because they lack a relationship with God, they may be even more dysfunctional. Do I hear an Amen?

Political Correctness and Public Policy

We can see how a caterpillar's nature directs him towards a doctrine of fairness and politically correct speech, but how does it manifest itself in public policy? Let's consider the issue of trying terrorists in our civil courts. The caterpillar liberals want the world to see that they can treat these cowardly perpetrators lawfully and fairly, so it has to be done in open court, even if these foreign enemy combatants could be tried just as judiciously in more secluded military tribunals. Caterpillar people are willing to risk revealing our national intelligence information and allow the terrorists to use the public hearings as a soapbox to spout their propaganda, or criticize America, so caterpillars can present a self-righteous image to the world. Since maintaining their image is crucial, they are willing to risk bruising the feelings of the 9/11 victim's families. Since other people determine their significance, they are a slave even to the opinion of our foreign foes. Like all caterpillars, they are compelled to try to earn the favor of people they do not even like, respect, or who have injured and killed their neighbors.

Our politically correct speech is also affecting our foreign policy, specifically our ability to deal with Islamic radicals. Liberals in our government and within the media hesitate to call an Islamic terrorist a "Muslim terrorist" because they do not want to offend moderate Muslims. Caterpillars believe the only reason Muslims attacked America was in retaliation because we had offended them so egregiously in the past. This false notion that Islamic radicals misbehave because we misbehaved first, stems from the self-centered caterpillar's psychological and emotional need for control. The Liberal Left believes that if they can change the Muslim world's attitude towards us by promising them no harm or treating them with greater consideration, they would *like* us again and halt their war against us. This sort of childish, immature, erroneous caterpillar thinking gives Liberals the false notion that they can control the radical Muslim's behavior through negotiation or manipulation. If we have ever negotiated a peace treaty without a conflict or a war, I can not remember it.

The truth is that we only have control of our own country, and even that is waning. No one can control the thoughts and behavior of another. The truth, according to the God of the Bible, is that as long as there are self-centered caterpillars, evil behavior will run rampant in our world. We must either defend ourselves against them or attempt to lead them to Christ, so they can be transformed into butterflies when He transplants His unselfish and peaceful nature in them.

Caterpillars See No Evil

Liberal caterpillars intellectually deceive themselves by adopting a false sense of responsibility for Jihadists' harmful behavior, rather than accepting the fact that there is evil in the world that lies beyond their control. If liberals acknowledged the evil religious, political, and military nature of Islam, then they would live in constant fear of them. They would rather assume this false cause and effect, and blame the Islamic terrorists' violent and despicable behavior towards us on American policies. Believing this lie gives them a false sense of control, which lessens their fear. From the caterpillar's self-centered perspective, they can not see the evil that naturally emanates from the Islamic religious and cultural worldview. Since they do not see radical Islamists as intrinsically evil, they underestimate their danger to America, which puts our nation's security at risk.

Islam is about controlling caterpillars, not about making butterflies! It is about oppressing people, not liberating them. Knowing this truth is critical as we continue to evaluate the true motives of radical Islam. Consider the American Muslim Imam, Feisal Abdul Rauf, regarding his proposed Cordoba Project, an Islamic center and mosque to be built near the site of the fallen World Trade Center Towers. His stated goal is to build bridges between cultures, yet Islam's militant history, brutal culture, and their self-centered worldview are totally contrary to the principle of tolerance and coexistence. Perhaps a recent "Letter to the Editor" I wrote would better explain the truth, regarding this proposed mosque.

In order to determine Imam Rauf's true intentions for the New York mosque, we must know why he calls it, the "Cordoba project." Cordoba was the name of the great mosque that was built on the foundation of a Christian cathedral in Spain after the Islamic invasion in the 8th century A.D. The caliphate of Cordoba was the first Islamic government in European territory, and the mosque at Cordoba was built on the same site as a previous Christian cathedral which marked their conquest. As a result of their victory, many indigenous Christians were sold into slavery, and the remaining people were ruled harshly until it was taken back in the thirteenth century.

Unlike Christ, who died to change the evil nature of man, Mohammed accepted that man had an evil nature. His numerous laws listed in the Koran were designed to be strict and severe, so Islamic government could rule with as little opposition as possible. Islam is more than a religion. It is a form of government that seeks worldwide domination and submission to their harsh and unmerciful Shari'ah Law. Islamic law is the antithesis of American law. It uses criminal means to control and punish immoral behaviour and immoral means to control and punish criminal behaviour. Unlike our "unalienable rights" that came from God, their laws came from man and are without equality for all.

The Cordoba mosque is not an olive branch to New Yorkers, but a "victory monument" to be built in the shadow of the Islamist's greatest triumph on American soil. It will serve as a beacon to every radical Muslim in the world that a foothold for the conquest of America has been established.

It is notable that the secular caterpillars in America and the radical religious Muslim caterpillars are both self-centered, yet neither group can see the evil that is ingrained in their own nature. **The reason this blind spot exists is that caterpillars, subconsciously, see themselves as the god authority in their lives. Since their impression of God is that He does not have an evil nature, then they can not possibly have an evil nature.** In addition to the caterpillar's self-centered worldview, there is a psychological reason a caterpillar has difficulty acknowledging the existence of evil in himself and the world. A caterpillar may serve as his own god, but he is still acutely aware he is only human. Therefore, he is incapable of comforting himself in such a dangerous and capricious world because, as a caterpillar, he has no more powerful God than himself to protect him from the evil that is inherent in our world. The caterpillar's life, the only life available to him, can be randomly snuffed out for no good reason at the hands of evil men. Unlike a butterfly, when a caterpillar dies, it means permanent death. Subconsciously, this is a terrifying way to live, so He tends to put blinders on to avoid seeing the evil that exists around him.

We butterflies can acknowledge evil because we are comforted by the all-powerful God who transformed us. Since we have placed our faith in Christ, we are victorious over the evil one because his caterpillar minions are powerless to separate us from the love of God or interfere with our salvation. Christ-followers can live with the knowledge that they can be the victims of evil at any time. Certainly, it would be sorrowful for those who remain. But for us, we are assured to return to our original home to Heaven to live in perfect health and peace for eternity. **Our world will never be free from evil until all men are transformed into butterflies that worship God, and God alone.** However, He reassures us that, in His time, He will be the one to conquer man's evil nature one caterpillar at a time.

Chapter Ten

God's Kingdom: America on Earth as It is in Heaven

In reply Jesus declared, "I tell you the truth, no one can see the kingdom of God unless they are born again."

John 3:3 (NIV)

"Suppose a nation in some distant region should take the Bible for their only law Book, and every member should regulate his conduct by the precepts there exhibited! Every member would be obliged in conscience, to temperance, frugality, and industry; to justice, kindness, and charity towards his fellow men; and to piety, love, and reverence toward Almighty God ... What a Eutopia, what a Paradise would this region be."

President John Adams

God sent His Son to rescue us from paganism and legalistic religions. He wanted to save us from living a self-serving, dysfunctional and hopeless life filled with the unhealthy consequences of serving unforgiving and inadequate gods, ourselves. This was Christ's initial ministry: to reconnect his caterpillars to God, The Father, by transforming them into butterflies that chose to place their faith in God, not man. In addition to saving us from ourselves, God wanted His butterflies to have His spiritual DNA inside of them, so they could truly call God, Father, and He could call them His children. He did not merely want to adopt his "new creations." He wanted them to be born directly into His family, which meant they had to

131

have God's Spirit within them. The only way to have God's spirit in them was to be born-again.

Jesus also had an equally noteworthy ministry that went beyond man's psychological transformation. This was political in nature. Once God transformed his lost caterpillars, He used the remainder of His newly created butterflies' time on Earth to strengthen their faith. As their faith grew, so did their obedience. The more obedient they became, the better they would be able to fulfill their responsibilities as loyal citizens of Heaven and reign with Christ in His coming Kingdom.

In God's Heavenly Kingdom, there are only butterfly citizens who love only one Father, serve only one King and worship only one God. Just as there was no room for more than one God in the Garden of Eden, there is no room for more than one King in God's Kingdom. Citizens of the Kingdom of Heaven must possess God's worldview, which is God is King, and they are not. In the Kingdom of God, all subjects are equally valued and loved by their sovereign Lord. Since everyone will be loyal to their King, no citizen will have his own agenda to compete against God's plans. They will be devoted to fulfilling His will, so peace and harmony in Heaven will be guaranteed.

If becoming butterflies makes us functional enough to be accepted by God and admitted to Heaven, then it is reasonable to assume that butterfly men should be the most functional form of man to live on Earth. **If it is necessary to live under the authority of God in His Kingdom, then constructing a government under God's authority should be nearly as effective on Earth as it is in Heaven.**

Our founding fathers wanted a form of government that reflected the nature and worldview of God's hand-made butterflies, not God's immature, larval caterpillars. America resulted from the dream of our courageous freedom-seeking, European, Christian pilgrims, and was founded by our bold and brave Christ-centered and God-honoring, colonial forefathers. They knew that butterflies made in God's likeness, would naturally desire to be obedient to God's will, while caterpillars would be willing to disobey Him and ignore His wisdom. These larvae would rebel against His authority because they believed that they knew better than God. **Our society was designed by butterfly leaders for butterfly citizens, who were to raise their caterpillar children to know the Bible, trust in God, and be transformed into butterfly adults. As butterflies, they would possess God's nature and worldview so that they could develop a functional, harmonious and peaceful God-centered, butterfly society.**

George Washington, who was a Christian said, "It is impossible to rightly govern a nation without God and the Bible." Hear the words of Samuel Adams, one of our more famous founding fathers, "Let ... statesmen and patriots unite their endeavors to renovate the age by ... educating their little boys and girls ... and leading them in the study and practice of the exalted virtues of the Christian system." Even the U.S. Congress declared in 1782, "The Congress of the United States recommends and approves the Holy Bible for use in all schools."

Our founders were overwhelmingly Christian, and those who were not Christian still believed in the providence of God and the tenants of Jesus Christ. For example, Thomas Jefferson, who had a disdain for Christian religiosity said, "I am a real Christian, that is to say, a disciple of the doctrines of Jesus. I have little doubt that our whole country will soon be rallied to the unity of our Creator and, I hope, to the pure doctrine of Jesus also." Jefferson also said, "God who gave us life gave us liberty. And can the liberties of a nation be thought secure if we have removed their only firm basis: a conviction in the minds of men that these liberties are the gift of God, that they are not to be violated but with His wrath? Indeed, I tremble for my country when I reflect that God is just; that His justice cannot sleep forever." Listen to the words Benjamin Franklin, when he interrupted the Continental Congress and said, "The longer I live, the more convincing proofs I see of this truth: that God governs in the affairs of men. And if a sparrow cannot fall to the ground without His notice, is it probable that an empire can rise without His aid?" An early American leader who did not have the God-centered world view was an anomaly.

Since we need butterflies in large numbers to create the most functional society possible, then the primary focus of our culture should be to encourage our citizens to develop a personal relationship with Christ, so they can obtain the Biblical, God-centered worldview. The functionality of a society is dependent upon it citizens adhering to God's Biblical moral virtues, which include personal responsibility, justice, charity, love, kindness, self-control and obedience to God. In order for citizens to cooperate well enough for peace to prevail, the caterpillar's previous self-centered nature must be transformed so that looking out for the well-being of their neighbors and upholding and preserving all of our "unalienable rights" becomes second-nature. Our forefather's dream for America could only come to fruition if American citizens became butterflies. **How can we expect caterpillar people to accept and adopt our forefathers' principle of God-given "unalienable rights" if they deny either the existence or the sovereignty of God who endowed us those rights?**

Our founding fathers desired that the Biblical worldview would become the philosophical cornerstone of our country. However, just as Jesus knew that not all people would answer His call to salvation, our wise forefathers knew that not all caterpillar citizens would be transformed into butterflies. Jesus taught, "But small is the gate and narrow is the road that leads to life and only a few find it." (Matthew 7:14, NIV) This means that in order for their new American society to flourish, they needed to ensure that their new government would not interfere with God's transformation of caterpillars into butterflies. Therefore, Article 1 of their new Constitution was to guarantee their citizens that the government would never come between its citizens and the free worship of God.

Jesus expected His butterflies to "be the salt of the earth … and light of the world." (Matthew 5:13-16, NIV) As salt, they were to preserve God's morality and the good and godly things in society. As light, they were to illuminate the truths of God's word, and be an example of God's love and goodness. We need butterflies to expose the evil that would overtake America if our caterpillar citizens reject or deny God and start munching away at our Constitution. Americans have had the privilege of participating in the only earthly experiment in Christ-centered government designed to imitate the Kingdom of God. For over two centuries, Americans have experienced the fruits of our godly founding fathers' representative republic, which has ensured its citizens unprecedented rights and freedoms. **Our forefathers understood that only a butterfly citizenry that operates according to God's morality could be trusted with these rights and privileges, and not subvert or abuse them.** Most of our colonial founders knew that Jesus is the Truth, and the truth shall set us free from tyranny; both from ourselves as individuals and from our government. They believed God's promise: those who honor God, God honors. The American system of government was made for a butterfly society, and at least for now, American butterflies and their larval caterpillars remain free!

Unfortunately, our American experiment is going sour because the nature of America is changing. Until the last fifty years, the majority of Americans held the Biblical, butterfly worldview and accepted living as one nation under God. Now, the numbers of American caterpillars have grown to the point that they appear to be overtaking the butterflies. **Our butterfly-oriented society is changing because the nature of so many American caterpillars is not.**

Untransformed caterpillars have led the political movement away from God and towards the man-centered philosophies of secular humanism, progressivism and socialism over the last century. These secular progressive caterpillars have been trying to keep Americans, young and old, from the transforming hands of Christ by enlisting the legal larvae of the caterpillar population to run interference for them. The ACLU, referred to by many butterflies, as the Anti-Christian Litigation Union, has been systematically attempting to remove any vestige of Christ and His transforming power from the public institutions of America. They have been as deceptive as Satan, as they slowly corrupted America's sense of Biblical morality and family values under the guise of protecting civil liberties. They have openly dishonored Jesus be subverting the true meaning of our laws, and disregarding the spirit and sanctity of our Constitution.

Secular progressives have been slowly plotting to take over America for most of the twentieth century. They believe that if they can prevent American citizens from obtaining or preserving our forefathers' butterfly worldview, they can change the nature of America and they are correct. These conniving caterpillars realized that without God intervening in the lives of their fellow larvae, there will be no more butterflies to interfere with their plans to trample the Constitution, restructure our economy, reshape our morality, and ultimately, control and oppress our citizenry.

Without the transformation of caterpillars into butterflies, lawlessness will prevail, and our country will implode like the Roman Empire. The rulers of Rome were pagan caterpillars, not Christian butterflies. Within a period of about 500 years, their culture crumbled because of declining morals, political corruption, over expansion of government, a failing economy and high unemployment of the working class. These same conditions are currently presenting in America after only a century of non-God-centered, Progressive leadership in America's federal and state governments. Unlike the Caesars of old, who were outright persecutors of Christians, our current President, Barack Obama, refers to himself as a Christian. However, based on his moral and political positions, particularly abortion, it is doubtful that he is a follower of Christ. He and his cabinet do not uphold and promote traditional Christian values and virtues, and certainly do not accept operating under God's authority. President Obama's stance on abortion is in exact opposition to God's. He sent no representative to the National Day of Prayer, yet he attended a Ramadan dinner.

If Barack Obama has undergone Christ's transformation, he must have been transformed into a moth that is afraid to come out of the spiritual darkness of his secular closet.

His numerous czars, with whom he surrounds himself, are not only untransformed caterpillars, they are proud self-centered progressives, or at least have progressive backgrounds. Neither President Obama nor his minions voice opposition to the ACLU, which is working incessantly to prevent our caterpillar population from becoming butterfly citizens. If they can remove the God of the Bible from America, there will be no more obstacles remaining to curtail immoral living and unbridled consumption of other people's hard earned wealth and property. **Whether the S.P. caterpillar strategy is a conscious or a subconscious one, it is simple. No more God, no more butterflies! No more butterflies, no more competition! Then, the country can be remade in their image.**

Life, Liberty and the Pursuit of Happiness

Before I discuss the meaning of "Life, Liberty and the Pursuit of Happiness" as it pertains to the goals of our republic, I want the reader to understand the meaning of these words as they are in the Bible. God created all life, and it is His to do with as He pleases. Since we can never purchase our lives from God, our lives will forever be the property of God and will never be our own. Likewise, the things people *create* or invent also belong to God, but He allows people to have complete control of their creations as their own property. However, unlike God, who will never part with His human creation, man can sell his creations to another person, and the buyer can make them his property to do with as he pleases. Human life belongs to God. It is His property. He will not sell it. From God's perspective, life and property are closely linked.

Liberty, which means freedom, is what man experiences when he knows the Truth, who is Christ. The Bible assures us that the Truth shall set us free from sin. Since sin is dysfunction, Christ will set us free from living in a dysfunctional state as a slave to the opinion of other people, and release us from the never-ending search for our own significance. Freedom, in the Biblical sense, does not mean freedom from God's authority, for it can only be truly achieved through submission to God's authority.

The way to achieve happiness is described in Psalm 119: 35 (NLT). "Make me walk along the path of your commands for that is where my happiness is found." We find our true and lasting happiness in obedience to God, and obedience is most easily achieved out of love for our Master. Love and joy, of course, can only occur within a relationship. It was God's perfect love that made Him perfectly faithful to us. Therefore, the more our love grows for God through our relationship with Jesus, the more faithful and obedient we will become. The more obedient we become, the happier we will be.

Our butterfly founders knew that "life, liberty and the pursuit of happiness" were the components of human existence that allowed man to experience his best possible life. Our founders listed these admirable goals in this order for a purpose. If our society does not place the protection and preservation of human life first, then insuring our God-given right to liberty means darned little, especially to dead citizens. If our government will do all it can to protect our lives, but it does not equally guard and maintain our constitutional liberties, our government will become our oppressors, and we will live under tyranny. If our government does not ensure life and liberty to all of our people, then there will be such upheaval and chaos, that there will be little chance for any of us to experience personal or societal happiness. We can not change the order of these noble goals of our American system of government without causing disorder in our society.

Recently, the Governor of Arizona signed a law allowing the members of law enforcement, in the course of policing their state, the ability to question people about their immigration status and made it a misdemeanor to be in the state illegally. As a act to protect the lives and liberties of its citizens and visitors, Arizona's government wanted to decrease the threat of illegal aliens smuggling people and drugs across the border. Its other purpose was to curb the rapid rise of murders and kidnappings by members of the Mexican drug cartels. In the process of attempting to protect Arizona's citizens, there could be a chance that American citizens of Hispanic descent may be mistakenly singled out and questioned regarding their legal status. Although protecting a citizen's privacy rights are extremely important, it does not compare to the preservation of the life of a citizen. An American citizen swears to abide by our Constitution, which specifically states that life comes before liberty. Therefore, a loyal American citizen of Hispanic heritage should adhere to the moral priority of our founders, and place the lives of his fellow citizens ahead of exercising his legal right to privacy. All of us do this in airports every day. Of course, if his rights are later determined to be purposely violated by the government, he is free to seek damages in court.

If our illegal immigration problems came from Canada, then Caucasians, like me, would expect to be occasionally inconvenienced and maybe even embarrassed by law enforcement in the name of protecting the lives of my neighbors. However, avoiding my embarrassment or humiliation, should I choose to take it that way, should never be a justification to deny our government's primary and legitimate mandate to protect the lives of my fellow citizens.

Jesus Christ should be our guide regarding the manner in which we view our legal rights. They are important, but they are not more important than the lives and well-being of our neighbors and our country as a whole. Just as Jesus was willing to temporarily suspend His divine rights to come to earth as a man, Americans should be inclined to defer some of our rights when it is appropriate. In Philippians 2:7 (NLT) it says, "instead, he gave up his divine privileges." He suspended his Godhead for the well-being and eternal preservation of His neighbor's lives. Jesus could better model the proper way a human being was to live and how he was to relate to his Father in Heaven. For Jesus, to live as a human being was not about securing and exercising His royal rights and privileges. It was about giving up the full privileges of God, so He could show us how to be fully human, and place the interests of others ahead of our own. **If Jesus suspended His role as God for a while to live as a man, then would it not seem logical that human beings would also have to cease being their own god, so they could live a human life with the same authenticity as Christ?**

Jesus elected to sacrifice his right to self-preservation and chose to die in order to preserve the eternal lives of His neighbors. Since butterflies have been made in the likeness of Christ, they also are responsible to preserve the lives of their neighbors for whom Jesus died, even if they must suspend their legal rights to protect them. Caterpillars demand their rights to protect themselves. They insist on exercising their rights, even if they place their neighbor's livelihood or life at risk. In the case of the Arizona immigration law, if one caterpillar person insists on exercising his individual right to privacy, it will increase the risk of having the law overturned. This may increase the chances that his neighbors or even members of his own family will be kidnapped or killed. How self-centered can a caterpillar get? When we view our Constitution from God's perspective, everything makes sense. When we do not, nothing makes sense.

Our caterpillar Americans are trying their best to forget that our Constitution was founded on Biblical, moral principles. Jesus believed the Law was made to serve man, not man to serve the Law. Yes, we are to obey our laws to the best of our ability, but if exercising our legal rights interferes with the government's ability to protect the lives of its own citizens, then it should remain in its proper place, second. **Our rights were endowed by our Creator to help us live long, abundant and fruitful lives. They were never intended to be worshipped above the actual lives of His people.** It is clear that caterpillars and butterflies see the world from the opposite perspective, which causes their interpretation and understanding of reality to differ greatly. I am not implying that the butterfly perspective is better than the caterpillar's perspective regarding government and a citizen's rights. I am declaring it so. **Of the two perceptions of reality, the butterfly worldview is true, and the caterpillar's is false, erroneous, wrong — a lie! One leads to peace and prosperity. The other leads to dysfunction, oppression and poverty.**

From the butterfly perspective, the key to making America and the world a better place is to transform as many citizens as possible so that the character of the majority of Americans resembles that of Jesus. The only way for this to occur is for butterflies to be able to freely spread the Gospel in public and private sectors of society. **Caterpillars must understand that living with Jesus at the center of their lives is the only functional way for human beings to live.** Once Christ has set them free from their caterpillar nature, they will have no further desire to live like caterpillars again. Now, butterflies can see that their previous caterpillar thinking was naïve, childish, somewhat nonsensical and extremely dysfunctional. Once they have been born-again into butterflies, they will rail against any attempt by their primitive, immature, liberal larval neighbors to corrupt or interfere with the butterfly's time-tested, traditional, God-fearing way of living.

If we butterflies do not act now, we will look back to this time in American history with considerable regret and sorrow. **How could we have stood by and allowed dysfunctional caterpillars to castrate Uncle Sam and turn him into the Nanny?** This is not the transformation God had in mind for America. My greatest concern is that caterpillars have been munching away at our Constitution for so many decades, there will not be enough of it remaining for us butterflies to restore. We need to rescue our Constitution from these caterpillars so that with God's guidance and power, we can resurrect our traditional, healthy American culture. Then we can restore America to President Reagan's "shining city on the hill" and

America can again be Christ's light to the world.

The Culture War Between Caterpillars and Butterflies

The difference in the nature and perspective between caterpillars and butterflies serves as the source of all human philosophical and political conflict. In fact, the culture war that is being waged in America today is between the post-modern, liberal caterpillars that have been "left" unchanged by God. They represent the American Left. The traditional, conservative butterflies that have chosen to be made "right" with God through Christ, represents most of the American Right. I say "most" because the Right is comprised of both God-centered butterflies, who have given Jesus the ultimate authority over their lives and God-oriented Christian, Catholic and Jewish caterpillars that at least acknowledge God's supremacy over man. They can see and accept the functionality of our founding fathers' Constitution because they acknowledge God's influence in its design and His active participation in the affairs of men.

The caterpillar Left is comprised of people with a self-centered nature including atheists, Humanists, cultural Catholics and Jews, Sunday Christians, and some non-Christians, as well. The hallmark of the caterpillar segment of society is that they have no subservient or loving relationship with God. To America's detriment, they have disregarded the authority and wisdom of God and our forefathers. They believe that their superior education and scientific knowledge are the keys to making the world a better place. They want to extend leadership positions to the most educated and intelligent rather than those with the most experience, character and integrity.

Liberal Progressive caterpillars live in communities all across America, and their way of life focuses on fulfilling their primal urges and desires. To our detriment, their self-focused nature makes them indifferent to the ownership of the gardens they consume or damage in the process. They want what they want, and they want it now. Their way of life is based on what others can do for them. Therefore, politically, caterpillars are natural-born opportunists. They have been waiting for a community organizer to move them towards a collectivist society sustained by the hard work of other caterpillars and butterflies. Caterpillars worship a *small* god, so they require a *big* government to satisfy their tremendous appetites and myriad needs.

The caterpillar, political Left knows that the best way to build and achieve their desired level of significance is to control the public coffers and secure positions of power. The most effective way for this to occur is to gain control of the media and primary and secondary education. They must be able to wield control over the masses in order for them to manipulate society for their purposes. This plan seems perfectly natural to caterpillars, since they already see themselves as the lords of their lives. They naturally view other people as inferior and consider their underling's interests less significant than their own. In fact, their superiority complex makes them think they know what is best for everyone. They also feel little or no guilt in taking the leafy treasure others have produced or earned, for they see it as rightfully theirs anyway. This is the psychological foundation for the Socialist's idea of redistributing income and property. Since caterpillars see themselves as their own god, they think they are intelligent enough to know what is best for America. **They believe they can and should control Americans, and they want to fundamentally transform our land into a new caterpillar country that operates as one nation under man.**

As I said before, butterflies need only a *small* government because they accept the fact that they live under the provision of a *big* God. Our founding fathers were butterflies, most of whom accepted Christ as their God. However, even the few who had not, such as Jefferson and Franklin, acknowledged that their new government represented one nation under the authority and sovereignty of God, not Man. Thomas Jefferson affirmed this belief and is quoted as saying, "A free people [claim] their rights as derived from the laws of nature, and not as the gift of their chief magistrate." The Constitution our founders penned reflected this core belief, and the limitation of power given to the federal government made perfect sense to them because it was consistent with their butterfly worldview. Jefferson also said, "I am not a friend to a very energetic government. It is always oppressive." However, no matter how persistent we are in trying to persuade caterpillars to accept the virtues of limited government, it is impossible for them to see our Constitution in the same light and from the same perspective as our butterfly founders.

Caterpillars believe they are far better educated and more knowledgeable than were our forefathers. Although this is untrue, they approach our Constitution as something for caterpillars to improve upon or an obstacle to be overcome rather than a sacred document that ensures our God-given rights and personal freedoms. In fact, caterpillars do not see our rights as "unalienable rights" from their Creator, because they either do not acknowledge God's existence, or they just refuse to submit to His authority. Since they choose to ignore the hand of God in the genesis of our Constitution, they believe it is subject to be changed by the only god they know, themselves. This represents the primary political perspective of the non-God-centered Progressive.

Some caterpillars have gobbled up "ivy" league, liberal propaganda and have developed an even greater superiority complex. They see the butterfly segment of our population as unenlightened, undereducated and backward beings. Even Barack Obama commented during the 2008 Presidential campaign that some Americans still cling to their "guns and religion." No authentic Christian, a genuine follower of Jesus, would ever chastise his Christian brothers and sisters for holding on tightly to God's Word. These puffed up super-caterpillars believe they deserve to govern and control all of the alleged inferior butterfly and caterpillar colonies.

Caterpillar politicians in government need power to maintain control over others. In order to solidify their positions of power, they promise their caterpillar underlings more and more free leaves in exchange for their votes. If they run out of leaves, they borrow some from foreign caterpillars or take it from their productive constituents by levying new taxes. They justify taking wealth from affluent caterpillars and butterflies because they believe the affluent cheated or unfairly gamed the system and accumulated just too many leaves. They sarcastically asked their fellow caterpillars, "How much money do they need?" Instead of rewarding successful Americans for producing food and creating jobs for caterpillars and butterflies, they promote class warfare and seek to penalize the producers. If left unchecked, the caterpillar leaders will make eating other people's leaves the law of the land. If this occurs, the property owners will lose control of the gardens they have worked so hard to cultivate. If the country remains under caterpillar control, there will be no gardens left to harvest for either caterpillars or butterflies.

Ironically, the same caterpillar liberals, whose real caterpillar counterparts survive by eating and destroying plants, are promoting the "greening of America" and fashion themselves as our ecological saviors. If they prevail in promoting this sham of man-made global warming and climate change, they will ultimately extract so many leaves from the American economy until the only green remaining will be the money lining the pockets of the caterpillar elite. The scientific evidence regarding global warming turned out to be nothing more than political philosophy espoused by liberal scientists. Those who promote a green America believe man has caused the destruction of the environment. Therefore, man must save it. It is the nature of a caterpillar to make false assumptions regarding the level of man's power and capabilities. He mistakenly rationalizes that man has created a near calamitous environmental situation. Therefore, if man caused it, then he must have control over its repair. **It is the liberal caterpillar's god-like image that makes him think he is capable of repairing something that an all-powerful God created.**

God has instructed butterflies to be good stewards of His creation. They know that as stewards, they are to care for and manage God's natural world. This means they are caretakers of the environment, not the creators of the environment. Man has limited control over the environment and, therefore, limited ability to restore the environment. Unlike caterpillars, butterflies have accepted the fact that Christ is the world's Savior, not Man.

Caterpillars also believe in conservation and protecting the environment, but they extend their reach too far by assuming they have the knowledge and power to save the planet. Caterpillars have a god-complex, and are working under the irrational belief that they are capable of saving an environment they do not thoroughly understand and can not recreate in the lab. They refuse to accept the fact that saving the environment is out of their control, or worse, is under God's (Nature's) control. Their intentions may appear honorable, but their leaders' self-centered nature will inevitably take over and corrupt their endeavor. Their compulsion to serve themselves will overwhelm them. It will be just a matter of time before they discover how to turn saving the planet into their personal, financial or political advantage. We can see this happening with the advent of trading carbon credits. These, "not so green" caterpillars, which includes our former Vice President, Al Gore, are in a position to make a ton of cabbage by procuring these trades, while never lowering the actual level of greenhouse gases they claim will kill our planet.

The caterpillar leaders' self-centered nature leads them to believe they have the intellect to outsmart everyone, including butterflies. In fact, they believe they are so knowledgeable and well educated, they are above adhering to God's general law of economics, which is: do not borrow more than you can repay. They believe that they are so unique and superior that living within a budget may apply to everyone else, but it does not apply to them. This is the same logic that every drug addict in the world employs. He knows that drugs are addictive, but he rationalizes that the drug's addictive properties do not apply to him. He thinks he is so smart and resilient; he will not get hooked. This thought process is immature and potentially deadly for America.

Since it is a caterpillar's nature to need the approval of others, they have considerable difficulty saying "no" to people, who have their hands out. If they remain in control of our government's finances, spending and taxing will never end. They will continue to take leaves from those with larger gardens, and redistribute it to those with smaller ones. They will suck the producers dry and turn the American landscape into a veritable desert devoid of any economic growth. Jesus offered to sustain His people with "living water," (John 4:10 NIV) yet America, the only Christ-centered society in history, will find herself choking on the dust left behind from the godless caterpillar's own sinful (dysfunctional) desires and self-indulgent behavior.

In addition to taking property from high income and wealthy Americans, the caterpillars will inevitably take more and more freedoms away from caterpillars and butterflies. They are well aware that their fellow caterpillars are earth-bound and can only see the mound of free leaves that government lays before them. They are blind to the oppression and tyranny of government that lies hidden behind the foliage, which will overcome them like a thief in the night. America is on the verge of collapse from within, but caterpillars are unable to see it. From the butterflies' loftier vantage point, they can see the erosion of our freedoms coming over the mountain of leaves the liberal caterpillars just took from them. **Again, Jefferson was well aware of this potential hazard of government when he said, one can "predict future happiness for Americans if they can prevent the government from wasting the labors of the people under the pretense of taking care of them."** Unfortunately, the liberal, left-leaning larvae, who quickly cited Jefferson's disdain for organized Christianity, have purposefully ignored his wisdom on other topics pertaining to government and economics.

In their zeal to become historically significant, caterpillars are so busy remaking America in their image, they do not seem the least bit interested in finishing their personal transformation into butterflies. In fact, they call themselves Secular Progressives, but they refuse to invite God to help them *progress* into the butterflies they were originally designed to become. These S.P. caterpillars are hell-bent on rejecting God's involvement and authority in their lives. They are unaware that it is not the caterpillar, but the butterfly, that experiences the more enlightened way of traveling through life. To butterflies, S.P. stands for Satan's People, for their goal is to thwart God's will in their individual lives and interfere with His work in the lives of their fellow citizens. They refuse to look to God for wisdom and insist upon relying on their over-rated caterpillar intellect. Their goal is to make America the best society of leaf-munchers possible, even if it means becoming a society of leaf-moochers in the process. This is the only way of life they can imagine because they do not possess the perspective to see the world in any other way.

Butterflies have an uphill battle ahead of them because they have no audible voices with which to raise their objections and caterpillars have no ears to hear it, anyway. It will require millions of butterfly wings waving in unison at rallies across our nation and during the next election campaigns to capture our caterpillar leaders' attention.

Liberalism: An Attack on God and the Family

The majority of caterpillars are evolutionists, yet they refuse to evolve into butterflies. They still see America as one nation under man, while butterflies that have been transformed by God naturally see their country as "one nation under God." Caterpillars know that in a representative republic, for them to take over our country, they must outnumber and outvote butterflies. The easiest way for them to achieve this goal is to prevent the transformation of caterpillar people into butterflies. Therefore, consciously or subconsciously, their strategy is to remove any evidence of Christ's presence from our history and our society. If they can insure that our caterpillar youth grow up unaware of Jesus, then our children will not look to Him for their normal transformation into God-centered butterflies. Caterpillars have been successful by promoting their liberal, Godless rhetoric in public schools and on college campuses all across our country. **With the help of the media, they have been indoctrinating our little caterpillars with heads full of mush into believing that man, not God, can make the world a better place.** As they educate these young minds, they implant and imprint their human-centered worldview in them. As a result of indoctrinating their students with their secular worldview, their students tend to get further separated from the reality of God and His moral authority.

As these collegians and graduates have families, God's influence and morality will tend to be less influential than the generation before. Our children, the parents of our future grandchildren, will more likely adopt the secular worldview introduced to them in college. Without Christ's transformation, their self-centered nature will grow unchecked by God's Spirit. The cohesiveness of a family depends on the selflessness of the parents, and selflessness is dependent upon becoming a servant to their families, not the lords of their individual lives. If Secular Progressives can prevent young adult caterpillars from becoming God-centered butterflies, the breakdown of the family will most certainly follow. In fact, it already has.

The "family" is the prized entity of God. He initiated and sanctioned marriage between a man and a woman, so they could start their own family. However, God's ultimate goal is to have parents and children become reborn as children of His family. Family is the group that represents the most integrated relationships available to human beings. Our Father in Heaven has lived with Jesus and the Holy Spirit, who represent His eternal family. God has only known family since the beginning of time, so it is understandable that the preservation of the family is sacred to God. Although each member of the Divine Trinity is one and the same, each has a different role to play in their close-knit family. They were so perfectly interdependent upon each other they functioned as one entity, the Holy Trinity. They not only shared life together; they became "The Life."

When God made Adam and Eve, they were immediately accepted as cherished additions to His family. They even played a role in God's family by tending the garden by day and spending time in fellowship with their Father in the evening, which further solidified their familial bonds.

The second reason I believe that God deemed the family to be the ultimate group relationship is because growing God's family was the primary reason for Christ's sacrifice on the cross. Jesus had to lose his life, so God's caterpillars that chose to believe in Him could be reborn as His butterfly children. They had to be made in the likeness of His only begotten Son in order for them to be accepted by their Heavenly Father and be incorporated into His family. Just like most things in God's reality, the death of Christ on the cross is also a paradox. In order for God's lost people, who were dead in their sin, to have life and reunite with their Heavenly Father, God's only begotten Son had to die. In nature, death must always come before life, no matter what the situation.

God made man to become members of His family. He wanted to love them just like any father wants to love his children. Our Heavenly Father wanted all of His children to participate in His Life, the life of God, and share in His joyful relationship with His original family, Jesus and the Holy Spirit. Only when the family is reinstated under God's authority, can the family optimally function and offer resistance and protection from the immorality of our caterpillar world.

Just as the cornerstone of God's family in the Garden was a strong, devoted and loving Father, God designed human families to have a strong, devoted and loving father, as well. Without a moral, principled and involved father in the family, his children will inevitably drift away from his influence and his God. The human family was designed in the image of God; a triune relationship. Mother and Father and Child represented the trinity of the family. Without Christ leading the family, it would be just a matter of time before the children will become adversely influenced by God's arch rival, Satan. In fact, it usually takes only two generations for the children to fall completely away from the influence of the Holy Trinity, and become slaves of the Human Trinity: Me, Myself and I.

The final reason I believe family was the most valuable thing to God is that it was the target of Satan's first offensive act against God. He tempted and enticed Adam and Eve away from the authority of their Father, not just to force them to sin against their Father, but to break up God's family. Satan knew from personal experience that if one defied God, one would be expelled from God's presence and His Holy family.

The result of Satan's disruption of God's family is that God's children will be forever influenced and directed by the Great Deceiver. Without being part of God's Holy family, they will become dependent upon their new father, the Father of Lies. These two deceived caterpillars were condemned to crawl behind their new leader, the serpent, Satan. However, they never became a true family unit because Satan was not interested in becoming their father. In fact, if the nature God is love, and Satan's nature is the opposite of God's nature, then Satan is the antithesis of love. Satan desires to have authority over his caterpillars, but unlike a real father, he is incapable of loving God's little larvae. Satan's original promise to us was for us to become like God, not to join his family. So, becoming a loving, cohesive family under Satan's influence is impossible. By allowing us to function as our own imperfect god, Satan knew we would inevitably begin to worship ourselves and become slaves to our own desires and urges. Satan's world is also a paradox. When he deceived us into becoming our own masters, he condemned us to become his slaves.

Today, Satan and his caterpillar minions are still working on his original assignment, which is to break up the family unit. The S.P. leaders in the media and our institutions of education and government have been inadvertently trying to weaken, unravel and redefine the family unit for a long time. These non-God-centered caterpillars move slowly and deceptively under the cover of darkness and they, like Satan, "prowl around like a roaring lion, looking for someone to devour." (1 Peter 5:8 NLT) They instinctively know that they can never control us like sheep until they can separate us from the protection of the Good Shepherd. It is difficult to disrupt an intact family that is held together by a strong father who is devoted to protecting and providing for his wife and children. It is so much easier to deceive and entice children from a broken or dysfunctional family into the immoral or criminal abyss. God, unlike Satan, supports his traditional families in the same way He partners with Christ-centered husbands and wives to hold their marriages together.

The key to maintaining a free society is to promote and secure the integrity of the family. Unfortunately, liberals in the past fifty years, wittingly or unwittingly, have been promoting their erroneous worldview, which has slowly led to the weakening of the interpersonal, familial bonds needed to maintain the integrity of the family. The Secular Progressives, starting with Margaret Sanger, who promoted abortion as a means of genetically purifying a population, has in the past century influenced Americans to diminish the intrinsic value of an unborn child's life. Some Progressives have campaigned to introduce and legalize drugs and pornography into society, which has created more conflict and disparate values in the family, making it much more difficult to raise children and maintain the integrity of marriages. They condoned and promoted "free love" in the 1960's, which led to more premarital sex, which resulted in more unwanted pregnancies and sexually transmitted diseases. Through legislation, they set up a marriage penalty in the tax code that makes it more financially appealing, in some cases, for people to live together as unmarried couples. Some sought to legalize prostitution, which will inevitably promote and condone infidelity that will lead to the dissolution of many more marriage and families.

Progressives are promoting gay marriage, which is their latest expression of flipping off God. Gay marriage represents a non-God-centered union that will be as dysfunctional as the caterpillars promoting it. Granting homosexuals the right of adoption will solidify the notion to their adopted children that it is acceptable to ignore God's laws and defy His authority, further weakening Christ's influence in the home. Secular Progressives are into granting rights, which according to our Constitution, only God can do. Sadly, there are too many caterpillars in America usurping God's role, and not enough butterflies to prevent them from trampling the Constitution and our traditional worldview.

Since the late 1960's, there has been a continuous degradation in America's traditional social values. The liberal caterpillars in Hollywood have moved the television portrayal of the father from "Father Knows Best" to father knows nothing. Dads are depicted as nerds, dunces, buffoons, and irrelevant members of a chaotic family that are easily manipulated by their children. In the 60's and 70's, the Women's Liberation movement encouraged women to pursue their individual careers to the detriment of the integrity of the family. Single women are adopting children, and being artificially inseminated in the hopes of getting pregnant without the prospect of that child ever having a father.

These events were promoted by people who had already given up on the notion of God, our Father in Heaven, so it is perfectly understandable that they also have diminished or ignored the earthly father's vital role in the family. If there are not enough dads remaining, who are willing to die to defend their children and sacrifice their lives to maintain their family, as Christ did to restore His children to His family, then our society will collapse. Just as God's children will experience eternal death without reconnecting with Him, so will the family unit die without a strong father. Without an intact family, unloved and neglected children will drift into gangs or cults in order

Only God Can Make A Butterfly

to experience a sense of family. If they have never experienced having a father provide for them, they will more readily accept their provisions from public welfare and other government programs. Gangs will use the fatherless in order to wield more power against authority, and self-centered, liberal caterpillar governments will use the fatherless to acquire more power to increase their authority. **Government welfare programs offer provision and dependency. Street gangs offer a sense of familial inclusion and protection for fatherless children. Unfortunately, neither is capable of loving them.** Progressive governments are operated by caterpillars, and being true to their nature, they seek to use these dependent people, so they can exert more power over the remaining caterpillar and butterfly families they have spent nearly a century trying to sabotage.

The American father used to be like the man paraphrased in the words of Alan Jackson's song, *Small Town Southern Man*; "And he bowed his head to Jesus, and he stood for Uncle Sam, and he only loved one woman, and was proud of what he had ...." Our founders' America expected the values and the morality of Jesus to be taught and reinforced in every home. They assumed that God would play a central role in the operation and function of our families. Without the influence of Christ, our families, which represent the fabric of our society, will weaken and disintegrate. In the past fifty years, two generations of self-centered, liberal caterpillars have tried to break down the family by removing God from its center. The Progressives will be successful in remaking America in their image if they continue to *progress* in separating the American family from Christ and removing our government from under God's moral authority.

The liberal caterpillar movement is more than an assault on traditional Americans. It is truly an attack on Almighty God. They want God out of the picture, so they can rule as our new god. Please do not misunderstand me. I am not suggesting that the Secular Progressives are under Satan's influence. I am declaring them so! If one is not leading people toward God, then one is leading them away from

Him. If one is not for God, one is against Him.

Below is one of my unpublished "Letters to the Editor" from 2009 which was a snapshot of our current American political landscape under caterpillar control.

> *In recent decades, caterpillars have grown in number and influence. In the 2008 general election, they broke through and were victorious in electing their long awaited community organizer, the King of the Caterpillars, Barack Obama. He is the caterpillar, for whom they have been waiting, to advance their non-God-centered, Secular Progressive worldview. President Obama promised He would fundamentally transform the American landscape. So, he has taken advantage of the near collapse of the credit and financial sector of our economy, and like any good caterpillar, he did not pass up the chance to let a "good crisis" go to waste and used it to gain more control over American citizens and their leaves. He has abrogated previous legal contracts to take over GM and Chrysler, and gave the unions a financial stake in these companies. He has his sights set on health care next.*
>
> *He and his caterpillar minions are using their many feet to sidestep or trample our Constitution. They also take every opportunity to kick to the curb nearly every traditional Christian value that has made America great. His caterpillar czars are working behind the scenes, munching away at our Bill of Rights, and his Caterpillar Congress is consuming every leafy greenback the U.S. Mint can print. They want to change the nature of our forefathers' butterfly country into something that makes sense to caterpillars and is consistent with their non-God-centered worldview. The King of the Caterpillars is so intently focused on remaking America in his image, that he can not hear our butterfly objections even if caterpillars*

had ears to hear. If this caterpillar administration is left to its own devices, our government will go bankrupt, our economy will collapse, and our American way of life will disappear. The only question that remains is, will the destruction of our country naturally result from their godless worldview, or will they do it purposefully?

What President Obama has done is truly remarkable! Although, caterpillars have no hands, He has managed to flip off our founding fathers and their God, and clipped the economic wings of our butterfly nation. In 2001, we were concerned that Al-Qaida terrorists might damage or change our American way of life forever. To my dismay, it is becoming more evident that, perhaps, we should be more concerned about Obama than Osama.

Today, we butterflies are watching in horror at the dismantling of two centuries of a Constitutional government and the traditional Christ-centered family. It is hard to imagine that as strong and resilient America has been throughout our history that we will be overtaken and destroyed from within by an infestation of caterpillars!

American butterflies must not be deceived into trusting caterpillar people when they profess that they also are religious and believe in God. Remember, even Satan believes in God! So, if it looks like a caterpillar and walks like a caterpillar, it's a caterpillar, and his government will reflect the same sinful and dysfunctional nature of the self-centered people who operate it. No matter how hard they try to paste benevolent butterfly wings on themselves, their government will be godless, dysfunctional and will inevitably become *too big* to succeed. If they can deceive and convince enough people that man's government can replace the provision of God, there will be hell to pay for our beloved country.

Chapter Eleven

The American Caterpillar's Creep Towards Liberalism

Woe to the sinful nation, a people whose guilt is great, a brood of evildoers, children given to corruption! They have forsaken the LORD; they have spurned the Holy One of Israel and turned their backs on him.

Isaiah 1:4 NIV

Whoever is an avowed enemy of God, I scruple not, to call him an enemy of his country."

John Witherspoon, Signer Declaration of Independence, Clergyman and President of Princeton University

Historically, before government leaders could establish a socialist form of government, public worship of God, specifically Jesus, had to be discouraged or eliminated. In Western Europe, which is now mostly secular, progressive caterpillars have been remarkably effective in removing God from the forefront of society. Since the 60's, many Europeans, from London to Amsterdam, have accepted the hippie mantra that "God is dead." In some western European countries the number of practicing Christians has fallen below ten percent. It is a shame that some of the most spectacular churches in the world are nearly empty. The Europeans have been so successful in eliminating God's influence and authority, most Euro-caterpillars have no idea that they are to undergo a metamorphosis to become

157

butterflies. There does not appear to be a culture war in Europe like there is in America, because there are not enough God-oriented caterpillars and Christ-centered butterflies remaining to put up a fight.

The Liberal's movement towards socialism in America has been slowly creeping along for decades like the caterpillars that have been promoting it. Caterpillars prefer socialism and butterflies prefer capitalism, because their individual worldviews dictate it. Our forefathers, who worshipped Christ or acknowledged the sovereignty of God, knew that the economy of the Bible was free-market capitalism, which is inexorably linked to the philosophy of personal responsibility. Christ is the Prince of personal responsibility. He left the responsibility to accept or reject Him totally up to the individual caterpillar. No other caterpillar or butterfly can make that decision for him, and God will hold each of them personally responsible until death if they reject His Son as their Lord and Savior. If they chose to live without God during life, then they can spend eternity without Him, as well. No exceptions will be made. God will not violate our free will. In other word, "If not God's will be done, then man's will be done."

As part of man's need to take personal responsibility for himself, God expects every individual capable of working to be responsible for earning a living in the marketplace and provide for his family. In the Bible, Paul reflected this sentiment of individual responsibility when he said in 1 Timothy 5:8 (ESV), "But if anyone does not provide for his relatives, and especially for members of his household, he has denied the faith and is worse than an unbeliever." He did not say that if society does not provide for each other's families they are worse than unbelievers. God commands each of His caterpillars and butterflies to give to the poor, not have their government to do it for them. Our liberal government's misapplication of God's command to feed the poor has adversely affected society for generations, because it had made the poor dependent. Secondly, this misinterpretation also may have led to a perverted understanding of Christian salvation called *collective salvation.* Christ seeks to reconcile each of His lost sheep to Himself on an individual basis, so each one could have a personal relationship with God. Thus, President Obama's understanding of collective salvation is totally unfounded, and if not corrected, will cause further misuse of government power and taxpayer money.

In Matthew 25:14-30 (NIV), the parable of the talents describes how God not only expects his people to provide for the family, He wants us to invest and accumulate wealth. The master gave three different amounts of money to three different servants. He expected each to invest the money to increase His wealth. The first two servants were successful in doubling his capital, and the third person did nothing with his share. Years later, when the master returned, he praised those servants who invested and doubled his money. But, when the master heard that third servant buried the money in the ground, he called him "lazy and wicked servant" (v.26) and told others to "throw him into the outer darkness, where there will be weeping and gnashing of teeth." (v.30).

It is clear that God wants us to earn a living and accumulate wealth, but He did not want us to worship money. He did not want us to live a life focused primarily on personal consumption as do caterpillars. He knew that materialism would lead to self-indulgence, which would become our greatest stumbling block in maintaining our connection with Christ. God wants us to make enough money so we can support our family and have a portion left over to give to the poor. He does not want us to hoard it for our personal consumption, for earthly treasure could be lost or stolen. He wants us to earn money in order to *give* better, not *live* better.

In the Old Testament, God expected man to give back a tenth of His money to His church, which was His people, not their religious institution, i.e. the Vatican. In the New Covenant, Jesus directs us to be "cheerful givers" with the money God entrusted to us. This tenant is consistent with a butterfly's nature, which is to feed on flowers and in the process pollinate them in order to produce new plants in the garden that will provide food for others to eat.

God gave those who had material wealth a moral imperative to feed the poor. He gave no moral imperative for the poor to receive it. This means that the poor are not entitled to other people's money. It is a gift. It is charity. God says He values a charitable heart, for as Jesus said in the first half of Matthew 26:11 (NLT), "You will always have the poor among you...." God knew that as long as man lived in a fallen world with natural and man-made disasters, segments of the human population would, at one time or another, live in poverty. He knew that there would be untransformed caterpillar people who would succumb to their sexual urges including homosexuality, promiscuity and adultery, and unhealthy desires such substance abuse, pornography gambling, etc. God also knew that people, who disobey Him in these and other ways will inevitably suffer harmful consequences, such as disease and infirmity, broken relationships, incarceration, and financial mismanagement; all of which may lead to outright poverty.

Once these hapless caterpillar people, who have not turned to God for their guidance and provision become impoverished, they will seek their provisions from other people. As they become accustomed to living off of affluent people's gardens, they will be less likely to ever live independently and will get fat, lazy and relatively poorer. On the other hand, as the highly productive caterpillars and butterflies are taxed more heavily, even the most productive caterpillars and butterflies will eventually become impoverished while the poor remain poor. When the affluent segment of our society gives directly and appropriately to the poor, the poor are sustained more efficiently, and perhaps, at a slightly higher level, while their generous neighbor's affluence remains intact.

God knows that as long as there are self-centered caterpillars that consume to excess and hoard leaves and immature butterflies that have not fully developed the charitable spirit of God within them, people will not give substantially to the poor. Consequently, our secular government's war against poverty is a foolish pipe dream. Waging this kind of war without God's intervention and direction in the lives of both the affluent and the poor makes it impossible for the healthy human psychological development necessary to become generous citizens, on one hand, and more responsible citizens, on the other. Every day we see some of the richest caterpillars being uncharitable, while the poor butterfly widow depicted in the Bible was generous to a fault, because that was her new nature. Caterpillar politicians appear compassionate as they promote and encourage the government to wage a war against poverty, yet they use other people's money to fight it. Individually, however, caterpillars tend to be much more miserly than butterflies when asked to donate directly to the poor and needy.

Only caterpillar people with a self-centered worldview, who think they are smarter than God, believe they can ever prevail in a war against material poverty. Even Almighty God knew it would be impossible in this fallen world. Christ came to heal the sick and minister to the spirit of the poor, not give them wealth. He knew, however, that a person remade by Christ would develop the courage and confidence to attempt to become self-sustaining and solvent. God expected him to rely on His power and guidance to overcome his individual circumstances. Christ wanted to reassure His people, that although they were poor, they were equally loved and as valuable to Him as any rich man. He wanted to convince them that even a poor man could be made rich by placing his faith in Him rather than in money. **Man's security and value are to be found in Christ, not in his bank accounts or retirement plans.**

A humble butterfly servant of God knows he not only needs to extend charity to the struggling poor, he needs to offer them Christ's spiritual food, the bread of life, the Gospel for their long-term psychological development and spiritual health. When Jesus reforms a person, that person becomes a new creation and receives the gift of the Holy Spirit of God to dwell within him. God's unwavering love for His new butterfly will motivate him to meet His expectation of personal responsibility, effective stewardship, and will help him become a cheerful giver of God's stuff. A butterfly's obedience to God will increase his chances of becoming healthy, wealthy and wise.

Not only do caterpillars have trouble sharing their leaves with the poor, they are so busy indulging themselves, sharing their time also does not come easily to them. Our caterpillar government needs to wage public relations campaigns to convince young caterpillars to serve, while butterflies are natural born-again servants who do it as a normal part of living. It is ironic that the same liberal, Secular Progressives in government who are removing Christ, the Creator of butterfly servants, are spending so much effort trying to convince caterpillars to act against their nature by serving in the American service programs. God is not seeking self-centered caterpillars that are occasionally generous with their time and money. He wants to make caterpillars into compassionate God-centered butterflies that naturally serve their friends and strangers throughout their lives.

There is not much any of us can do to change the American caterpillar's worldview regarding poverty, unless we can lead our caterpillar brothers and sisters towards a life-changing connection with Jesus. If we are successful in leading these caterpillars into a relationship with Christ, they will be transformed. God can reassure those with an impoverished spirit that they will not be alone in their uphill climb towards financial freedom from government. He and His butterflies will always be there to help lift them out of the depths of financial and emotional despair and remind them of God's promise of a new and abundant life.

The Liberal Way is Not God's Way

Liberal caterpillars are deceitful and duplicitous when it comes to introducing and promoting social welfare programs designed to help the suffering poor. In fact, these caterpillars appear to be exhibiting signs of a type of social Munchausen Syndrome. What do I mean by this? An example of Munchausen Syndrome is when a mother slowly poisons her child until the child becomes so ill the child needs mom's constant care. This caterpillar mother has an excessive need to present an image to her friends and family that she is the most devoted, caring parent to her child. Mom's self-image is so fragile, she purposefully chooses to harm her child, causing her own offspring to suffer, so she can receive the attention and accolades from others for being the dedicated, long-suffering mother. Since caterpillars innately believe they have no intrinsic value, she subconsciously or consciously, needs to bolster her low sense of significance and importance by presenting to the world this contrived image of a compassionate mother. She has perpetrated evil against her child as a result of her deep emotional need to make herself appear special to other people. Remember, the lower a person's sense of significance, the more likely they will be to hurt or use anyone to restore that image and the more evil behavior they will exhibit. Next to abortion and murder, this is the most evil, self-centered, trauma a mother can inflict on her child.

In the past five decades, liberal influence in our society has resulted in fewer citizens having the Biblical, God-centered worldview. Subsequently, there is more pathological human behavior in our society, which has led to an increase in moral decay, social injustice, economic decline and the erosion of personal responsibility in America. **Liberal governmental policies and programs, like the behavior of this emotionally and morally bankrupt mother, have disrupted our moral and fiscal health and caused our country to become ill.** Secular Humanists, Secular Progressives, Liberals, or whatever their current name de jour, are tying to make us believe they are overflowing with compassion by introducing sweeping legislation that will lavish benefits and entitlements on the jobless and impoverished masses. Unlike the mother in my previous example, they are unaware of the destructive consequences their policies have already had on Americans under their governance, but like the mother, they are hiding their dysfunctional, self-centered nature behind an image of benevolence. They also try to deflect their dysfunctional worldview by blaming their opponent's fiscal policies for the exact problems they caused through the imposition of their godless, pathological understanding of the role of government. These caterpillar congressmen and women are even more despicable than the mother, who at least expended her own time and effort to offer relief to her suffering child. Liberal caterpillars, within both parties, shamelessly add insult to injury by funding their "nanny state" programs on the backs of the same Americans who have been suffering from their dysfunctional political ideology and misguided morality. Now that's evil!

When it comes to adjudicating punishment in our culture, it bears repeating that untransformed caterpillar people value fairness, while God and His butterflies value justice. Being a just person is a measure of a butterfly's character and integrity. They understand that making the guilty and irresponsible people pay the consequences of their behavior will result in their personal, psychological and social benefit. A man needs to possess the character and integrity of God in order to do what is best for the other person and society in general, especially when it is a difficult and sometimes an unpopular thing to do. In fact, God treats all of us this way. He does what is best for us even if it is inconvenient or painful, because He is more concerned with our character than our comfort. **For butterflies, having a just character is most important!**

As I said before, caterpillars need to be liked. Therefore, they need to relate to others in fairness, for exhibiting justice may prevent other people from liking them. The measure of caterpillars' personal value is measured by how much others like and approve of them, which determines the way they feel about themselves. This is their nature, and they are slaves to it. As a result, our unsaved caterpillar brothers have a difficult time accepting the fact that some people are justifiably suffering from their own irresponsible, immoral or criminal behavior. Caterpillars would rather attribute another person's failings to society's corrupting influence. In this way, they will not be seen as cruel people, who insist on making these offenders pay the consequences for their own misdeeds. They need to present themselves as the savior of the downtrodden and underprivileged. They tend to behave like overindulgent parents, who make their son's bed, so they do not have to punish him for ignoring his responsibility. Rather than insisting that their child behaves responsibly, they rescue him from his responsibility because, above all, they want their child to like them. **For caterpillars, being a likable character is most important!**

Caterpillars need people to like them so much, they will do just about anything to keep the laziest and most irresponsible citizens in our society from suffering the just financial consequences of their behavior. Liberals will lie to themselves, so they can purposefully misinterpret the reason for others descent into poverty. These caterpillars would rather characterize these impoverished people's misbehavior as misfortune than have someone think badly of them. Psychologically, caterpillars are compelled to consider these people to be victims, so they can avoid the responsibility to inform them that they must endure the unpleasant consequences of their self-induced poverty.

I am not denying that some people may have been victimized or suffered a legitimate hardship that resulted in their financial decline or collapse. These people, however, represents a small minority. Regardless, liberal caterpillars can not tolerate the disparity of wealth between the haves and have-nots, because their self-serving nature dictates that they need to appear nonjudgmental and caring. It is their non-God-centered worldview that determines their belief that life is supposed to be fair. This false perspective on life causes them to despise wealthy individuals and profitable businesses and corporations. Since they see the affluent and wealthy business owners as criminal perpetrators of the poor, they are willing to absolve the poor from any significant responsibility for their plight. If liberal caterpillars were to attribute the suffering of the impoverished to poor decision making, immoral behavior, or irresponsible spending, they would be required to take responsibility for judging and rehabilitating the poor. That would place their likable image in jeopardy. A caterpillar is driven by the emotional payoff that will inflate his sense of significance.

Liberal caterpillars believe that redistribution of wealth will level the playing field between rich and poor, because if this disparity was left unchanged life for some would be **unfair.** The ultimate benefit of promising redistribution is that it will make the poor see these self-centered liberals as their benefactors. These caterpillar politicians are savvy enough to know that they merely need to present the image of being their benefactors in order to earn their votes. This means that entitlements must be announced with fanfare, so the voters can be aware of their compassion and generosity. Unfortunately, the disastrous result of giving away the tax-payers money is that the beneficiaries have become a dependent class, and will be less likely to take responsibility for their financial future. Less responsible adults create more dysfunctional and broken families, whose members are more likely to commit immoral and harmful behavior, which will permeate our communities and inevitably infect our entire country.

As long as caterpillars need to feel good about themselves, the actual effect their policies have on our country remains secondary. Caterpillars may appear to have a "bleeding heart" for the disadvantaged, but because of their self-centered nature, they will inevitably use them to advance their personal ideologies and political aspirations. Have you noticed that as often as caterpillars promise to transfer leaves to the less fortunate in our society, the poor get poorer and the under-performing population continues to expand? The sad truth is that in our society, these self-centered liberals' primary focus is to be perceived as our saviors. Consequently, they believe they should be evaluated on their noble intentions rather than their successful outcomes. After spending trillions of dollars on their war against poverty, the citizens they intended to help are still struggling, and the liberal caterpillar offers their standard explanation that they have not spent enough money. They will not accept personal responsibility for the failure of their policies and will always blame poor outcomes on someone or something else.

Government handouts and entitlements are not God's ways of providing for our individual families or our struggling neighbors. God created us to love our neighbors as ourselves and commanded us to care for the widows and orphans. **God did not create government on the eighth day to replace Man's charitable heart!** Throughout history, governments were usually the purveyors of oppression and evil, not the bastions of charity to the poor. In fact, governments more often than not, starved their subjects through exorbitant taxes or outright thievery. God expected the individual citizen or citizen groups to share a portion of their bounty with the poor. God did not designate government to replace the individual's responsibility to care for his struggling neighbor.

When government usurps our God-appointed role of giving to the poor because it has taken our extra money in taxes, it undermines the butterfly's ability to respond wholeheartedly to God's command to feed his sheep. When individual citizens voluntarily give to the poor, it binds the affluent and the poor together. This interaction allows the poor and less affluent members of society to know that their more financially secure neighbors care about them. In this way, the poor can learn to recognize the rich as their helpers rather than their oppressors. When government gives entitlements to the poor, it officially separates the wealthy Americans from the poorer Americans, which results in the belief that the wealthy somehow have created their poverty. The liberal politicians use this unhealthy psychological illusion to promote class warfare and divide America so that they can utilize this schism to gain political power and control. The modus operandi of the caterpillar is to divide and conquer.

Caring for the afflicted and trying to provide our hurting or struggling neighbors with money, housing, clothing, food or moral support is *my* civic duty as an American and *my* moral duty as a follower of Christ. However, God does not expect our charity to elevate their economic status. It is merely to sustain their lives and allow those in need to experience the love of God through the generosity of His butterflies. Hopefully, this expression of God's love would have a life-changing, spiritual impact on the lives of the underprivileged that might inspire them to work their way out of poverty. Our generosity will reassure them that we represent a helping hand to lift them up rather than an iron fist to beat them down.

The proper role of government is to defend our lives and to uphold our unalienable rights endowed to us by God. It is not to extract other people's money through taxes, so it could transfer it to the poor as a grand gesture of compassion. Unfortunately, in our politically correct society, the disagreement regarding the role of God in government has not only impaired our ability to defend our God-given rights, we are beginning to lose them. **How can a liberal government be counted on to protect the rights given to us by God, if that same government is prohibited by its own courts from proclaiming God's name and influence within the institutions of government and the public domain? Our Constitution was clearly designed for butterflies, not caterpillars.**

People who love God have a natural desire to be obedient to His Word. God knows that if we voluntarily and cheerfully give our stuff away to those in need, it will give us the best feeling about ourselves that we could ever experience in life. The more frequently a butterfly expresses his love for his neighbor, the easier it is for him to give away his love the next time. The more love a butterfly gives away, the bigger his heart becomes, and the more pleasing He becomes in the eyes of God. This is the cycle of love that results from possessing the healthy psychological attitude and worldview needed to generate the giving spirit in God's butterflies.

Butterflies are designed to exhibit God's just nature, which means they expect people to reap what they sow. However, they also possess God's merciful and loving nature and are the emissaries of God's love in our world. Butterflies are expected to extend forgiveness, mercy, grace and generosity to others whenever possible. Once a butterfly has been loved by God and received his wings that will carry him to Heaven, worldly things tend to dwindle in importance compared to his knowledge and love of God. Since butterflies have experienced the life-changing power of Christ, they eventually will love God more than money and become more generous with their own wealth.

Unlike caterpillars, whose value is based on their power, position and possessions, a butterfly's value is not measured by how much he owns, but who owns him. A butterfly knows his true value is equal to the price God paid for him, the life of His only begotten Son. According to butterfly people, character is revealed by doing good works when no one is watching, because they know God is always watching and will be pleased. God desires us to have the proper motivation, so we can give cheerfully to those in need. He wants us to give, because we love the poor as ourselves, not because we pity them. The struggling poor are our neighbors, and we believe their lives are equal in value to our own regardless of their financial status or social position. We donate generously to them, because they are our brothers and sisters. Becoming disadvantaged like them may be just one illness, accident or lay-off away. Butterflies tend to give charity anonymously, because they are not to impress other people with their gifts. God reinforces this notion when He tells us in Matthew 6:4 NIV, "that your giving may be in secret," desiring no earthly adulation or rewards, because we will receive our reward in Heaven. Giving in secret allows butterflies to focus on improving the lot of their neighbors rather than improving their image to their neighbors. **The caterpillar gives until he feels good about himself. The butterfly gives until the poor no longer need his help or he has nothing left to give.**

Giving something freely to another person without an expectation of a return is called *love*. When caterpillar politicians create government policies that transfer tax money to certain citizens, they usually expect a financial donation or a vote in return. Politicians do not love; they trade. This fine philosophical line between barter and bribery is often blurred. When government takes our money and gives it to those in need, they determine the ones in need. Under these circumstances, we butterflies would be fools to think that self-centered caterpillars, whose nature it is to serve their own interests, would direct government aid to the truly needy rather than their political cronies, party supporters and business associates. Fortunately, butterflies are no fools. The are well aware of the caterpillar's self-serving and deceptive nature, because they used to be caterpillars. **Why would an American butterfly ever trust caterpillars to exhibit the just character of God, when they have already ignored or rejected His desire for their transformation?**

If the caterpillar style of politics prevails, this wrong-headed form of compassion will eventually discourage producers, which will result in our country's economic collapse. Once our country is significantly weakened, they or our conquerors, will be able to impose a tyrannical government that will control and oppress all Americans. Instead of America being the purveyor of goodness in the world, she will become the exporter of evil. If this downward trend continues, we will collapse from within, and America will fall like the Roman Empire did centuries ago. Whenever I reflect on the caterpillar's worldview regarding poverty, I think of the words attributed to one of my favorite preachers, the late Adrian Rogers.

> *"You can not legislate the poor into freedom by legislating the wealthy out of freedom. What one person receives without working for, another person must work for without receiving. The government cannot give to anybody anything that the government does not first take from somebody else. When half of the people get the idea that they do not have to work because the other half is going to take care of them, and when the other half gets the idea that it does no good to work because somebody else is going to get what they work for, that my dear friend, is about the end of any nation. You cannot multiply wealth by dividing it."*

God designed His creatures to be free. However, there can be no freedom for God's children if government interferes with its citizens' ability to earn a living or attempts to control the fruits of their labor. Citizens can not be generous with their money if the government controls their businesses (fascism) or the fruits of their labor (communism). Since proper stewardship of God's resources is His command for every butterfly, one can not be a faithful steward of God's wealth if a government entity can seize control of personal property and dispose of it with little or no accountability to its citizens. It is logical to conclude and consistent with God's Word that having property rights is an unalienable right from God. For God's butterflies, there can be no real freedom under any form of socialist, collectivist government. In fact, according to my analysis, there can be no freedom without capitalism and no capitalism without freedom. Frankly, when it comes to capitalism and freedom, neither can be sustained by a society that refuses to live under God's authority.

Chapter Twelve

A Caterpillar's Choice – America's Destiny!

"Yes, they knew God, but they would not worship him as God or even give him thanks. And they began to think up foolish ideas of what God was like. As a result, their minds became dark and confused. Claiming to be wise, they became utter fools.

Romans 1:21-23, NLV

"There is not a truth to be gathered from history more certain, or more momentous, than this: that civil liberty cannot long be separated from religious liberty without danger, and ultimately without destruction to both. Wherever religious liberty exists, it will, first or last, bring in and establish political liberty."

Joseph Story, Congressman and Supreme Court Justice

If the caterpillar represents the immature, dysfunctional form of man, then a self-centered caterpillar government "under man," i.e. liberalism, socialism or communism will be just as dysfunctional. The Liberal Left wants to change the nature of our country by trying to control the behavior of caterpillars and butterflies. God's way of changing the behavior of our caterpillar countrymen is to change their nature by transforming them into butterflies. Our founding fathers expected American caterpillars to choose to be transformed into butterflies, just like God had transformed so many of them. They expected Jesus to change the hearts and minds of young caterpillar Americans, so they could develop a society that reflected the character and personality of God. Butterflies realize that our founders' experiment in Christ-centered culture and limited government not only makes sense, it is preferable over any other. Ultimately, we must preserve it if Americans are to remain free.

Butterflies, as I said before, are the more functional form of human beings, so their society and form of government will also be more functional. If God's desire for human beings is to travel through life as butterflies, and the liberal caterpillars have done all they can to remove Jesus from the landscape, then any society designed and controlled by the Liberal Left will totally ignore or selectively adhere to Biblical values. If secular, self-centered caterpillars continue to control American politics, then our country will sadly end in moral decay and social chaos, for their government must reflect the godless nature of its leaders. It will be just a matter of time until their liberal government becomes so bloated trying to be everything to everyone that America, as we know her, will be crushed under the weight of her own debt.

Caterpillars rationalize to themselves that they can ignore God's Biblical laws and build a country outside of the will of God. When caterpillars *rationalize* their plans for America, they, unwittingly are telling themselves and us *rational lies*. **Caterpillars who do not know the Truth (Jesus) can not see that their premise for understanding the world is false.** Unfortunately, until a caterpillar develops into a butterfly, it will be impossible for caterpillars to see that their assessment of reality is a lie. This is so frustrating for butterflies, because they can see the lie since Jesus, who is the Truth, lives within them. Regardless how many examples we present to caterpillars, they will remain blind to the truth.

Conservative radio talk show hosts Rush Limbaugh, Sean Hannity and Glenn Beck acknowledge the supremacy of God over man, and have been teaching, explaining, and presenting eloquent and logical arguments for many years, regarding the reasons liberal caterpillar doctrine is erroneous, nonsensical and harmful. Yet, in 2008 the Liberals won the presidency and the majorities in both houses of Congress. In my opinion, these intelligent and persuasive men are beating a dead horse trying to convince liberal and S.P. caterpillars to see things from a butterfly's perspective. **Trying to explain the benefit of adopting conservative values to a caterpillar is like trying to describe America's colors of red, white and blue to a blind man.**

Since it is impossible for an earth-bound caterpillar to have a butterfly's worldview, then why waste time trying to convince a caterpillar to behave contrary to his nature? Why spend years trying to get a caterpillar to adopt conservative principles that are totally foreign to him, when a butterfly that possesses God's Biblical worldview will understand and adopt it naturally? **If these conservative media icons want our citizens to see America and the world from their perspective, they would be infinitely more effective by preaching the Gospel. It will be our citizens' submission to Christ, not conservative arguments that will transform liberals into conservatives.** If we expect to have any hope of restoring our country to "one nation under God," as our forefathers intended, we have to introduce our fellow caterpillars to the same God who transformed our founders into butterflies over two centuries ago. The cure for what is ailing America is to encourage more caterpillars to seek Christ and be transformed into butterflies. I know it seems odd that a political cure is dependent upon a spiritual awakening among Christians and all Americans, but it is true. **In order to make America soar again, we need more butterflies. And only God can make a butterfly.**

Today, in American politics, it is as if the lower, less mature form of man is taking over our country. President Obama and the Secular Progressives want to remake our butterfly America into a country that is consistent with caterpillar values and needs. Their goal is to transform our land, our "butterfly conservatory" that so many Americans love, into one that has no flowers, no fruit, no cocoons

— just lots and lots of green leaves. Our President is willing to reject the dream of our forefathers in order to transform America into his image. He is willing to munch away at the fundamental freedoms guaranteed in our Constitution, and defy God's desire for him, personally, to become a butterfly.

President John Adams said, "Our Constitution was made only for a moral and religious people...." The morality to which he refers, is God's Biblical morality, and this morality is reflected in our Declaration of Independence and Constitution. In it, our founding fathers offered Americans many freedoms that are not available in other countries, because our government system was designed for butterflies, whose behavior was already internally governed by God. In contrast, caterpillars that are not internally governed by God need many more restrictions on their freedoms to ensure an orderly society. Whether they are secular or religious, caterpillars require a more heavy-handed government (Socialism, Communism, or Islamic Shari'ah Law) that externally governs and controls their self-centered, dysfunctional behavior.

In this regard, liberal government is similar, but not exactly, like an Islamic caliphate. **The primary difference is that Islamists are trying to control moral behavior by forced adherence to Islamic Law, while Liberals are willing to justify immoral behavior through purposeful misinterpretation of Constitutional Law.** Take the ACLU, for example. They cite our freedom of speech and privacy, and twist its meaning to justify the legalization of pornography and abortion. This manipulation of the First Amendment certainly does not represent our forefathers' Biblical values and is a perversion of our founders' true intent. **Thomas Jefferson warned us of this potential to distort the law when he said, "Laws are made for men of ordinary understanding and should, therefore, be construed by the ordinary rules of common sense. Their meaning is not to be sought for in metaphysical subtleties, which may make anything mean everything or nothing at pleasure."** The most famous example of using metaphysical subtleties to parse ordinary language occurred in President Clinton's impeachment, when he said, "It depends on what the meaning of 'is' is." Caterpillars will do or say whatever it takes to get their way or to save their behinds.

Unless the majority of our citizens are butterflies, they will ignore God's morality. In fact, liberal caterpillars will create their own morality, and will change it anytime it suits them. If the evil nature of America's caterpillars is left unchecked, they will be free to distort and pervert existing law or create new laws to insure the loss of our individual freedoms. It will be merely a matter of time before America experiences the controlling and oppressive type of government that has plagued the Muslim world for over a thousand years.

Since the nature of a caterpillar is to control others, then there can be only two classes of caterpillars in their world: those in control and those to be controlled. Just, as in the Islamic world, our caterpillar leaders desire to control the remainder of the population, yet they want little or no restraint on their own behavior i.e. sweetheart deals, comprehensive, blue-chip health insurance, and adulterous affairs, etc., for they see themselves as being members of the ruling class. Their natural sense of superiority will justify allowing other citizens fewer freedoms than themselves. **The liberal and Islamic psychological propensities for oppression and tyranny are a direct result of their self-centered, caterpillar worldview.**

For caterpillars, the freedoms in the Constitution must be ignored or deceptively removed, because the majority of the American population will never voluntarily allow Congress to legislate the loss of their unalienable rights. In order for other caterpillars and butterflies to be controlled, the government needs to intrude more deeply into their personal lives. Liberal caterpillars also work to promote more economic dependence upon government in order to gain control over the masses. Fortunately, our Constitution has a Bill of Rights that limits what the federal government can do to its citizens. However, secular progressives and President Obama have been suggesting a new Bill of Rights, which will delineate what the government *can do* to its citizens, and how it can legally control the behavior and property of Americans. Butterflies that are already governed by Christ can see the government's incremental attempt to limit their freedoms, and from their loftier viewpoint, they can see the disaster that is in store for America. Butterflies repeatedly warn caterpillars that their policies will strip us of our liberty. Yet, from their lowly perspective, they just can not see the danger the future holds, and they invariably think we butterflies are alarmists, or even worse, bigots.

Caterpillars value man's knowledge above God's wisdom. They have it in their minds that they are smart enough to build a socialist, collectivist's utopia that is superior to God's system of capitalism and individual rights and responsibilities. Like all self-centered people, they are hell-bent on achieving their progressive ideas of building a nanny state, even if the American economy nearly collapses and our people get hurt in the process. In fact, Progressives realize that it is easier to take over the private sector if they weaken our economy first. Since caterpillars are psychologically driven to get their own way, they have no difficulty bending congressional rules or purposefully sabotaging the opposition's efforts to re-establish our traditional values and capitalist economy. Only dysfunctional caterpillar people would risk collapsing their own country in order to remake it to suit their needs. In essence, Liberals are trying to do exactly what God does in a caterpillar's cocoon. They are trying to dissolve the core values and moral structure of America in order to make our country into a new creation. Caterpillars see themselves as the god-figure in their own lives, so it is natural for liberal political leaders to assume that government also plays the role of God. **Therefore, it is natural for them to utilize government to transform America into their image. Unfortunately for America, they are trying to transform a butterfly nation into a caterpillar commune.** They must win this culture war by any means possible, because maintaining their superior image depends upon it.

It is unnecessary for Liberals to be exceptional leaders, because they are willing to govern against the will of the people. They merely need to be persistent and single-minded in their effort to nudge American caterpillars in the direction they desire until they reach their destination. **True leaders, like Jesus, inspire people to follow them. Self-centered Liberals behave like all tyrants and simply push people around.** Here, is a recent example. Our administration rammed through a health care bill against the will of the majority of Americans. They pulled all the legislative tricks available to them and offered their fellow Democrats exorbitant bribes in order to pass this tax bill disguised as a health care reform bill. Apparently, liberal caterpillars wanted to provide government-sponsored health care even if it kills us, which the escalation of health care rationing will do to some Americans. Butterflies can see from God's perspective that the caterpillars' attempt to transform our country into one that fits their nature and image will be regressive, oppressive and dangerous. Yet, caterpillars are blind to it. They can only see what lies directly ahead of them, and they are salivating at the impending tax hikes and the redistribution of leaves from upper-income earners and the wealthy into their bottomless bellies.

Our caterpillar Liberal Left is so self-serving and intent on eliminating Jesus from the hearts and minds of Americans, they again remind me of the ancient Pharisees. In their zeal to rid the country of Christ's influence and limit the conversion of Jewish caterpillars into butterflies, Pharisees plotted to murder Jesus in order to maintain their control over Israel and her people. I can hear Christ's words echoing in my mind, pleading with His Father, "Forgive them for they know not what they do." (Luke 23:24 NIV) Caterpillar liberals do not realize that as a result of rejecting Jesus and America's Christian worldview, what remains of the good moral character of our society will disappear, and America will slide into a cesspool of evil and anarchy. **These self-focused caterpillars do not realize that they have been the beneficiaries of living in a decent and orderly society because of America's Christian butterfly ethic and morality. It is the Christian tenet that every person's life is valuable that made American society the open and tolerant**

society it is today. When you think about it, secular caterpillars have been freeloading in our Christian society for decades. They have been the beneficiaries of our country's moral goodness and decency because American butterflies' promoted and adhered to our Biblical and Christian values. Moral goodness does not come from self-centered caterpillars. It comes from God-centered butterflies. Liberal, non-God-centered progressives have abused America's God-endowed freedoms and privileges by sabotaging and subverting the same Christian foundation that provided all of our freedoms in the first place. It is as if these secular progressives are fish trying to poison the water in their own lake. Caterpillars would rather continue to deceive themselves that they are the lords of their lives and create chaos in their own country, than submit to God's authority and risk losing their perceived power and control.

No Pain! No Healing!

The best and most relevant illustration regarding how a caterpillar's worldview is detrimental to our country is occurring now, in 2011, as Congress attempts to correct our massive annual budget shortfall. Their pitiful, yet comical attempt to balance the budget shows how a caterpillar's worldview determines his choices and approach to real life challenges. Let me set the stage. The Democrats in Congress have offered to cut the budget by $6 billion and the Republicans want to trim $61 billion from this year's deficit. The leader of the Senate Democrats says that he wants to use a scalpel to delicately trim the budget, so the people who are depending on government assistance will not suffer. The Republicans insist this cut in spending is a paltry sum and will have no significant impact on the deficit. They, on one hand, want to be sensitive to the pain trimming the budget may cause some American citizens. Yet, on the other hand, they want to show us that they truly grasp the seriousness of our country's fiscal dilemma. So, they made a bold offer to cut $61 billion, which to me, is still an insignificant amount. If the problem is a $1.6 trillion annual deficit, then cutting $6 billion or $60 billion is no answer.

Each political party's impotence in balancing America's budget has little to do with their differing understanding of governmental budgets or their lack of accounting skills, intelligence and ingenuity. Their ineffectiveness is due to their shared worldview regarding something much more subtle and fundamental. **Their worldview of the human condition assumes that *pain* is unacceptable and should be avoided at all costs.** This is certainly not God's view of pain. If His son, Jesus, had to endure excruciating pain to complete His mission, then we should assume that pain and suffering is a natural part of life. God gave us the sensation of pain to let us know something is physically or emotionally broken. We are not to mask or avoid pain. We are to call upon God to lend His wisdom and power to help us face and endure our pain, while He guides us to take the proper steps to address our brokenness. However, without a relationship with an all-powerful God, caterpillars can not see the role of pain from God's perspective. They can not see pain as a warning sign to seek help from a benevolent God, because they have no God to help or comfort them. To them, pain is merely an agonizing condition of the body or mind that interferes with their self-focused pursuits. Therefore, the logical conclusion for caterpillars is that pain is unnatural and unnecessary to the human experience and should be eliminated from their lives.

It is the caterpillar's non-Biblical attitude towards pain that is the stumbling block to achieving a balanced budget and making our country healthy again. These Congressional caterpillars have placed America's financial solvency in jeopardy. Their self-centered perspective caused them to believe that if their government was to solve any of our problems, it should not involve inflicting pain or suffering in the lives of their constituents. Their governmental and personal creed is in stark contrast to the physician's creed to "First, do no harm." This oath does not direct physicians to avoid causing any pain. If they avoided causing pain, very few of their patients would ever get well. It was the caterpillar's misinterpretation of the role of pain in our lives that resulted in the over-expansion of the government's social, medical and welfare programs, which created our massive debt in the first place. Therefore, it is pure fantasy to think that we can correct such a monumental budget imbalance without expecting all Americans to experience significant pain.

The worldview of our caterpillar leaders and legislators makes it impossible for them to see that the liberal distribution of other people's money has not reduced the suffering of America's poor. After decades, the impoverished and middle class are still struggling, and now the entire country is on the brink of bankruptcy. These wrong-minded politicians in both parties desire government to play the role of a protective nanny in the lives of Americans. However, the truth of the matter is that liberals in government are undermining the health of our country and corrupting the lives of the very people, to whom they want to appear compassionate. It is either their ignorance or denial of God's morality that makes caterpillar liberals a significant source of America's hardship and suffering.

In order to explain how the liberal's pathological avoidance of pain makes life worse for all of us, I would like to use the example of a patient with severe neck pain. John complained of neck pain radiating down his left arm shortly after a sneezing spell. The doctor found John's neck x-rays to be abnormal, so he ordered an MRI, which showed a slightly ruptured disc in the lower part of his neck. The doctor prescribed narcotics for pain until a neurosurgeon could perform an operation to relieve the pressure on his compressed nerve. The patient kept his appointment with the surgeon, but refused surgery because he did not want to experience the post-operative pain and risk other possible complications of surgery. So, the doctor sent John for physical therapy and continued his pain medicine. After six weeks of physical therapy, he was not much better. John was still taking narcotics, but now he was taking them five times daily instead of three as prescribed. The surgeon offered to perform the corrective and curative surgery, but John declined again, since the narcotics were masking much of his pain. The neurosurgeon warned him that he was becoming addicted to the narcotics, and not to wait much longer to undergo surgery. John did not return.

During this time, John lost his job due to repeated absences. He was fired from his next job, because he failed a drug screen for narcotics. He struggled financially and was quickly going into debt. He soon lost his home and resorted to selling his furniture and other personal belongings, so he could buy his drugs on the street. John borrowed money from everyone he knew to maintain his habit. When he was nearly broke, he went to his doctor one more time to get a prescription for pain pills, because it was cheaper in the pharmacy than on the street. However, it was obvious to his doctor that he was addicted to the narcotics, which he initially prescribed for temporary pain relief. He referred John to drug rehab, but John did not want to go through the pain of withdrawal.

In time, John found a steady supplier of illegal narcotics on the street. Occasionally, he would wonder if he should have surgery, and he even told his drug dealer he had changed his mind and decided to undergo the operation. Each time he mentioned having surgery, his dealer would respond by telling him that he would never be able to handle the pain of surgery or drug withdrawal. The drug dealer did not dissuade John because he wanted him to die. He just did not want the patient to recover because he would lose control of him and his money. The dealer pretended to be concerned and compassionate by reminding him of the many terrible things that would happen if he underwent the recommended surgery and drug rehab. If John had been reassured that he could endure and survive the pain of neck surgery when he was first injured, he could have avoided the dysfunctional life of addiction, chronic pain and poverty.

Liberal caterpillars behave just like drug dealers. They need their constituents hooked on welfare and public entitlements. They will fight against any plan that might free people from their dependence on government and make America healthy again. They are godless caterpillars and can not behave contrary to their nature. They need our nation to be broken, and our people indebted to them or they risk losing their control, power and significance. The last thing they desire is for someone to convince dependent Americans that they can survive without their monthly financial fix.

The Liberal establishment has, and will, mercilessly attack anyone who attempts to heal our government's financial woes. They will accuse any politician who offers a plan to cure our bankrupt country of trying to inflict unimaginable pain and hardship on the public. They will even suggest their true intention is to kill unsuspecting Americans. Politicians who think they can heal America without causing significant pain and sacrifice are thinking only of themselves, not their fellow Americans. These self-focused, liberal caterpillars are the source of America's prolonged pain and suffering, and if they are not defeated, they will become America's executioners, not her saviors.

Christ is at the Core of American Values

The economic and moral problems that exist in America are not due to lack of technology, productivity or education. They exist because not enough caterpillars have been transformed into butterflies. Since our caterpillar politicians must earn their significance, their political life is focused on getting favors to gain power and giving favors to gain control. Their emotional and psychological need for control makes them susceptible to greed and corruption, which undermines their ability to remain honorable and trustworthy public servants.

Our country must be led and governed by butterflies that reflect the character of Christ, because they have an internal moral guide who will remind them to put others before themselves. Nearly two hundred years ago, John Jay, America's first Supreme Court Justice, promoted the election of Christians to government when he said, "Providence has given to our people the choice of their rulers, and it is the duty as well as the privilege and interest of our Christian nation to select and prefer Christians for their rulers." I have repeated this quote because I truly believe the survival of America depends on having butterfly Christians at the helm of the ship of state.

The rationale for this statement is that man can not serve two masters, himself and God. The Christian butterfly serves God because that is his new nature. Those who serve God are able to love their neighbors as themselves, because they are capable of putting the interests of their neighbors ahead of their own. Since a butterfly's significance has been determined by God, he does not need enormous power and wealth to boost his self-image. It makes perfect sense to me that the people we want in control of the country's coffers are people who do not need money or power to define their own significance. Followers of Jesus do not constantly need to earn the praise of their constituents, for they already have God's affirmation. Therefore, butterfly representatives are less likely to be corrupted by the power of the purse, and are better able to focus their efforts on serving their countrymen instead of their own bids for re-election. **In order for us to trust our leaders, we must know that they truly trust in God. The phrase "In God we Trust" printed on our currency reminds us that our individual and collective security depends on having God in our hearts and minds, not money in our pockets.** Our founders designed America to be led by butterflies because they knew it was the optimal way for American society to thrive and survive.

Since Jesus was at the center of Creation, He was to be at the center of every one of His people's lives. Our founders held this worldview and surmised that a citizen who possessed the character of Jesus would make a wonderful law-abiding citizen, because after living under Christ's authority, living under the authority of a butterfly government would be accepted as natural. To quote Daniel Webster, an early American statesman and Constitutional lawyer, "Whatever makes men good Christians, makes them good citizens."

Without God guiding and governing the behavior of our citizens, our forefathers' experiment in a representative republic will fail. Our second President, John Adams said, "There are two educations. One should teach us how to make a living and the other how to live." Our early American school teachers emphasized Biblical study in every child's education, so they would know how to conduct their lives. Children even learned to read by reading Bible verses out of *The New England Reader.* The reason our citizens need to be guided by God's wisdom is two-fold. The first is personal. A God-centered person is a more content person and a more responsible citizen. The second reason is political. Self-centered, butterfly citizens will tend to elect other butterflies that will respect and comply with our Constitution.

From reading the Bible, we know that if God's spirit does not reside in man, nothing good can come from him, for only God is good. It is clear that without God in control, America will reel out of control. Just like everything else in God's world, governing is a paradox. **Only when individual Americans give up their personal self-rule to God will they be able to develop a government worthy and capable of self-rule.** The greatness of America has been due to America's belief in God and the adoption of the Biblical worldview. Therefore, it should be no surprise that America's demise will come from her rejection of God and His absence from the hearts and minds of the American people.

America may be at the end of her run as a super-power, and without a major Christian revival, our beloved country will soon collapse from within like every other Christ-less culture has throughout history. Fortunately, there is still a glimmer of hope for American culture. The Secular Progressives have been wrong about many things over the past century, but their greatest erroneous assumption was that "God is dead!" They could not be more wrong. God is not only alive, He is living here among His creatures and His Spirit resides within each of His butterflies. As followers of Christ, we understand that our last remaining weapons against Satan and his stubborn caterpillars are the freedom to spread the Gospel and the power of prayer. As long as these two things exist, America has a chance to survive, for "with God anything is possible." (Matt. 12:26 NLT) It is God's nature to forgive, transform and save those who respond to His call and surrender their lives to Him. We butterflies must dedicate ourselves to do God's will by spreading the Gospel to the millions of spiritually hapless, handicapped American caterpillars. Remember, Christ sacrificed His life for caterpillars, not butterflies. Then, God can begin transforming and reviving America one caterpillar at a time.

It should be clear to all butterflies that it will not be logical arguments, advertising campaigns or physical force that will save America from our caterpillar brethren. It will be God's love through a relationship with Jesus that will change the hearts and minds of our self-centered caterpillars. Only when Americans become butterflies will they be able to see and understand God's unwavering truths and appreciate the unique historical significance of our American experiment in representative government. **Caterpillars will never fully respect and value our forefathers' Constitution and their vision for America until they respect, revere, and submit to the authority of the God who inspired its creation.** Trying to convince the caterpillars of the Liberal Left to honor the sanctity of our Constitution and understand the benefits of small, limited government is like trying to convince real caterpillars that unbridled consumption of leaves is not in their best interest. It's impossible!

Truth and Lies

It is the self-centeredness of caterpillar governments and the absence of Christ's influence in their regimes that serve as the foundation of Liberalism, the hallmark of Socialism, and the genesis of all evil leaders and oppressive governments around the world. For example, Hitler denied Christ! Stalin denied Christ! Mao denied Christ! Bin Laden denied Christ! The list goes on and on. Find any political group of mass murderers or genocidal governments and the common denominator will be the absence of a relationship with Jesus, as well as, the denial of the Biblical worldview in the lives of these cruel dictators and ruthless regimes.

We butterflies are to defend ourselves against evil men and

governments, but only the power of God can conquer them. God tells us butterflies to put on the armor of God to defend against self-centered men who possess the same nature that dominated and enslaved us as caterpillars. God has the option to use his limitless power to subdue them, but I believe His true desire is to transform them. In many sermons, I recall hearing, "We do not need to pray for God to take our side. We need to pray for Him to take over." Only when caterpillars accept that our benevolent God still exists and is in control, will they ever voluntarily submit to His authority and allow Him to change them into butterflies that possess His just, loving and peaceful nature.

We human beings will never be able to experience the peace of God "that surpasses all understanding," (Phil. 4:7 NIV) as long as we remain caterpillars that get to determine what is true and what is false. If each person serves as his own god, there may be as many as six billion gods in the world; each believing that he or she has the correct truth. In this scenario, truth is in the eye of the beholder and becomes relative. As long as there are billions of individual caterpillar gods, all wanting to have things their own way, there can be only conflict among people, whose self-centered nature compels them to impose their version of the truth on their neighbors. Relative truth is merely a lie masquerading as truth. Living according to a false understanding of the world will always lead to personal psychological conflict and a pervasive, immoral, and dysfunctional society.

Our moral code is a value system that defines our conduct, and if it is to be proper and righteous, it must come from a perfect being. Only God can determine absolute truth and morality. Since there can only be one truth to a single reality, and Jesus is the Truth, we have to see reality from Christ's butterfly perspective in order to know the truth. The truth is found in a person, not our learned assessment of reality. **For caterpillars, the truth is relative. For butterflies, the Truth is our relative.**

John 8:32 (NIV) says, "Then, you will know the truth, and the truth will set you free." It does not say anything about man *learning* the truth. No one can learn the absolute truth of our world regardless of the depth of one's education, investigation, or experience. *Knowing* comes from developing a close relationship with the Truth, who is Jesus, so He can personally reveal to us the truth regarding our value, purpose and the proper understanding of the world He made for us. **We human beings mistakenly think we must learn the truth before we can know the truth. God says we must know the Truth (Jesus) because it is impossible to learn the truth.** Jesus came to testify to the truth by revealing Himself to us. There is no truth to be found in science, medicine, philosophy or government that does not come from God or lead us to Him. Since Jesus is the Truth, then living according to His God-centered worldview will allow man to lead his most functional life. If a person lives according to Man's self-centered worldview, he will condemn himself to live a dysfunctional life. **In other words, the butterfly's worldview is true, and the caterpillar's worldview is false!**

In the last fifty years, America and the world have been suffering from "truth decay." The Secular Progressive caterpillars, Satan's People, have been trying to force feed us "settled science" such as evolution and global warming that leaves God out of the equation, and "revisionist American history" that leaves Christ's influence out of America's story. If Jesus is Truth, and the caterpillar Left has ignored or rejected Jesus, then they remain children of the Liar, Satan.

Since the foundation of the liberal caterpillar's worldview is a lie, any logical conclusion they may reach regarding how to improve America will not only fail, it may result in the corruption of what remains good and honorable in our country. Without being transformed by Christ, they will see a lie as the truth. In Isaiah 5:20, he refers to this phenomenon when he said, "Woe unto them who call good evil and evil good…" Whoever rejects God's authority will inevitably see evil as good and good as evil. For example, several decades ago, most traditional, God-centered Americans considered abortion to be the murder of the unborn and the most heinous act committed against a woman and her baby. Now, our caterpillar society considers abortion a reasonable and acceptable act while they accuse pro-life butterflies of being oppressors of women's rights. Butterflies, like God, hate the act of abortion, not the people who have one. Caterpillars view abortion as a personal and appropriate right, but they consider those who oppose it as hater's of women. **Butterflies hate the *sinful act*. Caterpillars hate the *people* who want to prevent their commission of the sinful act.**

According to our Constitution, God endowed Americans with the unalienable rights of life, liberty and the pursuit of happiness. Whenever one unalienable right competes with another, such as life versus liberty, God expects us to seek and apply His wisdom in His guidebook, the Bible. It is quite clear that God never intended for us to exercise the right of our personal liberty to choose abortion at the expense of another's right to life. The problem with making a judgement about our God-given rights outside of His parameters inscribed in the Bible is that some people will exercise their unalienable rights at their whim for their own benefit, thus subverting or interfering with their fellow citizens' unalienable rights. Instead of using God's unalienable rights to help us maintain a just and orderly society, godless people will selfishly abuse those rights and cause confusion and dysfunction throughout American society. When individuals reject the Lordship of Jesus and the sovereignty of God, they will suffer the personal consequences of their incorrect, self-centered worldview. **When a significant portion of a country's population ignores or rejects Christ and fails to adopt God's Biblical worldview, they condemn their society to suffer from moral decay, cultural degradation, government corruption, economic collapse, civil unrest, and inevitably, civil war or foreign conquest.**

In general, if anyone who espouses something as truth, but ignores, rejects and dishonors Jesus, or that belief is contrary to

God's Word, you can be darned sure it is a lie. The best example of how caterpillars try to disseminate lies as truth is to compare our Constitution to the 2010 Health Care Bill. Our Constitution was written by butterfly men and is less than twenty pages long. Truth can be described openly and succinctly. False doctrine and deceitful lies must be cleverly camouflaged. The House's health care bill was written by caterpillars and is over 2200 pages long. It takes many pages to covertly remove our freedoms, disguise new taxes as health reform, and cleverly define moral behavior such as abortion under the guise of guaranteeing medical coverage. Our country is in peril because the Liberal Left has propagandized and deceived our caterpillar citizens into believing that they could create a properly functioning society and operate a beneficent government outside of God's authority.

God knows that if you are not working with Him, you are working against Him. If you are not walking with Him, you are moving away from Him. Caterpillars that directly or indirectly work to keep their brethren from a transforming relationship with Christ work against God, and are doing Satan's bidding in his eternal battle against God. The Apostle John described Satan as "the Father of Lies" (John 8:44 NIV) and "the accuser of our brother" (Rev. 12:10 NIV). Satan's job is to corrupt everything that is good. Therefore, regardless how noble or beneficial America's larval caterpillars' intentions may be, they base their decisions on man's understanding of the way the world operates rather than God's. Since caterpillars do not live according to God's worldview, no matter how well educated and intelligent they may be, they will create a dysfunctional America doomed to failure and destruction. **Truth and function go together, just as falsehood and dysfunction go together.** Living according to God's worldview will allow man to know the Truth, live according to the Truth, and introduce others to the Truth.

These constantly munching caterpillars have been devouring our wealth, eating away our freedoms, and spitting on our Christian values for decades. If our caterpillar neighbors continue to resist and reject Jesus, they will never receive God's gift of their butterfly wings and America will never soar again. In fact, these prideful caterpillars will use their millions of legs to trample our Constitution and, in the stampede to gain control of our leaves and our lives, they will reduce our country into the dust from which we all came. In order to reduce the amount of truth decay and eliminate the foul odor emanating from the mouths of these clueless caterpillars, we butterflies must increase our efforts to spread the Gospel and make disciples of all nations. We must do everything we can to re-establish The Truth, who is Jesus Christ.

Our country is teetering on the brink of self-destruction. If we are going to be serious about making disciples of all nations, let's start with America. We butterflies realize that nothing worth doing is ever easy. We have a difficult job ahead of us, because faith in Jesus comes through hearing the Gospel and caterpillars have no ears with which to hear. To make our task even more difficult, butterflies have no audible voices. However, our perfect God has not left us helpless. He has given us beautiful wings to attract our caterpillar neighbors out of the darkness, and His loving heart to draw them towards the everlasting arms of God. He has given us the humility and the desire to fold our wings in prayer for God to transform our lost caterpillar brothers and sisters. The resurrection of America is literally in the healing hands of God, the Great Physician.

Only the adoption of the God-centered worldview by the majority of our citizens can prevent America's transition into Socialism and tyranny. We must lead our wayward caterpillar citizens to Christ, so God will again bless our beloved country. **In order for this to occur, we must stop being closet Christians. We are not moths! We are butterflies!** We need to make ourselves more publicly visible and exhibit the love of Christ more frequently. We want the transformation of caterpillars into butterflies to become so desirable that even the most stubborn and rebellious of caterpillar atheists, cultural Catholics, social Christians, and other lost religious people will start their journey towards a transforming faith in Christ. If even half of the Christians, who accepted Jesus as their Savior, would also accept Him as their Lord, the Christian worldview will again prevail in America. In time, these new butterflies could help us lift America out of the hole that Satan's caterpillars have been digging for the last 50 years. **The only way the nature of our country can be changed is for God to change the nature of its citizens, one caterpillar at a time.**

If I could print a warning sign on my butterfly wings, it would say: No Christ! No Constitution! No Country!

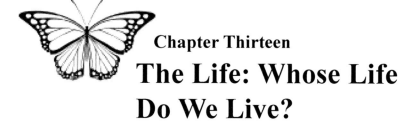

Chapter Thirteen

The Life: Whose Life Do We Live?

So you also are complete through your union with Christ, who is the head over every ruler and authority.

Colossians 2:10 (NLT)

"I am a real Christian – that is to say, a disciple of the doctrines of Jesus Christ."

Thomas Jefferson

Although I am extremely interested in the salvation of my country, I am most interested in showing people the truth about their own value to God and the truth of the reality of the world in which they live. Once they know these truths that can only be found in a properly oriented relationship with God, they can begin to live functional, fulfilling and more meaningful lives. Unfortunately, even believers are constantly affected by the immoral and unhealthy attraction to this world, and they need constant correction and guidance. This is why God sent His spirit, the Holy Spirit, to live within us to be our helper. I assumed for many years that God gave Him to us, so He could live His life through His newly transformed butterflies. As I have matured, I see that this notion still reflected the remnant of my old self-centered nature and worldview. If you think about it, God does not need me or anyone else through whom to live His life. I need Him in order to have life and properly live it.

Jesus claimed He is "The Life." He did not merely say that He was the first life, or He would improve our lives, or give us a new life.

He also did not say, "I am *a* way, *a* truth and *a* life," as if to infer that he was just one of many gods. He is the One! Jesus boldly and emphatically said, "I am *the* Way, *the* Truth and *the* Life!" Could Jesus have literally meant what He said? Is He the only one who has a Life? Do we live our lives through Him or does He live His life through us?

Since Christ transformed me into a butterfly many years ago, I have been diagnosed with cancer, and by His grace, He has kept me cancer-free for over ten years. Just as God can turn evil into good for those who love Him, He used my experience with cancer to teach me more about Him and His ways. I have taken what I learned from my bout with lymphoma, as well as, treating hundreds of others with cancer, to develop a cancer-cell analogy to explain whose life we truly live. Allow me to employ a simplified medical illustration regarding the function of cancer cells to depict our self-centered, malignant nature and how Jesus transforms us wayward, cancerous cells, so He can incorporate us into His body and participate in The Life of God.

Most people think cancer cells are fundamentally abnormal or deranged cells that invade other organs, and when they kill enough healthy cells, causing those organs to become dysfunctional, the patient becomes ill and dies. The truth is that cancer cells are anatomically and physiologically normal. If they were not operating properly, they would be ineffective cells and die long before they did any damage. **Malignant cells are normal cells that have become dysfunctional because they have strayed from the control of their *parent* cell.**

A cancer cell is created when some carcinogen, i.e. virus, chemical, etc. compels the cell to break free from its parent cell's control, losing the ability to follow its genetic instruction and perform its intended function. Cancer cells do not destroy our bodies because they misfire or malfunction. They behave exactly according to their new nature, which is now self-focused and self-directed. These cells have broken their relationship with their parent cell, and they do not perform any function other than reproducing and having their way with our organs and other tissues in our body. Cancer cells are self-centered, doing what they want, and doing it to excess wherever they are. In this way, they behave a lot like caterpillars.

Cancerous tumors are composed of living cells, but they do not have a life. They could never exist as a separate entity without a living host, for they are totally dependent upon their host's cells to provide them with oxygen and food to grow. They have declared their independence from their parent organ, yet they have become more dependent than ever upon their neighbor cells for their survival. They are now programmed to serve their own desires, and they do not care if their previous partners, their neighbor cells, get damaged or killed as a result of their unrestrained consumption and replication. In the process of behaving without proper direction or boundaries, these cancer cells will inevitably damage and destroy the lives of so many neighbor cells; they will ultimately cause the organ to fail. When they metastasize, they will invade other organs and inevitably kill their host, causing their own death in the process. Cancer cells are intensely self-focused. They do not realize that behaving in such a self-defeating manner will lead to their own demise. **If cancer cells had brains, we would call them "fools!" If they had a conscience, we would call them "evil!" If they had a name, we would call them "mankind!"**

People who live outside of our Divine Parent Cell's authority and control are just like these cancer cells, "evil fools." We are perfectly designed organisms, who do not need to malfunction to misbehave. All we need to do is live our lives outside the control and guidance of our spiritual parent, God. As distant progeny of Adam, we have no innate knowledge of God, our original Father, so our true purpose is unknown to us. Neither, are we sure how to behave in a healthy, functional manner. We tend to behave just like cancer cells, consuming, but never feeling satisfied. Our instinct drives us to satisfy our physical urges and fulfill our psychological needs even if,

197

sometimes, it is to the detriment of others. **Since we live outside our Creator's control, we live out of control and create unnecessary pain and suffering for ourselves and those with whom we come in contact.** Our self-serving nature compels us to want what we want, and want it now, and just like cancer cells, we do not seem to care who gets hurt or damaged in the process, not even ourselves.

Humans are living beings, but just like autonomous cancer cells, they can never truly have their own lives while separated from God. Since all people are born without a relationship with Christ, their desire to be their own boss comes naturally to them. Just like cancer cells, caterpillars assumed that being their own boss was the best way to live, when actually they were ensuring their own deaths.

We humans are so intelligent, yet our decisions are often emotionally driven and are determined by our feelings rather than our God-given logic and reason. As smart as we may be, we do not have a clue that living as our own god condemns us to a slow suicide. What we consider living is nothing more than existing until we die. This understanding supports the Biblical truth that we are born "dead in our sin" (Eph. 2:1), we just do not realize it. Living outside the authority of God is sin, and "The wages of sin is death." (Rom. 6:23)

The cancer cell had a relationship with its parent cell before it broke away, in effect, taking control over its own life as if it were its own god. Since we humans never had any congenital knowledge or connection with God, we do not become dysfunctional. **We are born dysfunctional! Our destructive and evil nature is congenital.** This means that our psychological, emotional and physical health and well-being is adversely affected from birth. Our erroneous perspective on life results in pathological behaviors, which become more prevalent and more destructive the longer we remain outside of God's control.

In order for us to function properly again, we must be brought under the authority and control of our Creator, Almighty God, so we can learn His purpose for our lives and the proper way to relate to others.

Our Creator is the only one who knew our original purpose and proper function, so He is the only one who can redirect our lives in the optimally, healthy way that He intended.

So, let's return to the original question. What does Jesus mean in John 14:6 (NASB) when He proclaims, "I am the way, the truth, and the life; no one comes to the Father but through me?" As I have shown earlier in this chapter, Jesus is the only way to be reconnected to the Father, our parent cell. In fact, Jesus does more than just help us search for the truth or even find the truth. He is the Truth. Only after we make Jesus our Lord and enter into a relationship with God through Him, could we know the truth of God's direction and purpose for our lives. **The truth lives in Jesus, and in order to know the truth, His Holy Spirit must live in us. Without God first living in us, He can never transform our malignant nature and make us acceptable to live in His body, the body of Christ.** The Holy Spirit only will be sent to live in us when we accept Jesus as our Lord and Savior. He is our true God, and we can only know the truth about ourselves and the world around us after we surrender and entrust our lives to Him. Only through faith in Jesus can we experience the abundant life on Earth that God promised us.

Though it is true that God uses man to do His will, He does not live His life through us. **"I am The Life" means God is the only Life that will ever be!** This means that throughout all of eternity, there was only going to be just one life for humanity, His Life.

It is one thing to be alive. It is another to have a life! It is certainly true that God breathed life into us, but He did not make man, so he could spend a lifetime separated from Him. His plan was to transform us so that we could be reunited with Him and become involved in His Life, the Life of The Holy Trinity, the Life of Our Creator and Almighty God! He is the Only Life that exists now and for all eternity!

When God created man, He crafted us in His image as a triune being having a mind, body, and spirit. This is a perfect representation of the trinity: the mind, represented by the Father, the heart, represented by Jesus, and the spirit, represented by the Holy Spirit. In order for a human being to have The Life, they would need to possess all three. Yet, Jesus promised to send only part of the Trinity, the Holy Spirit, to dwell within us. In order for us to be in The Life, we must be a part of the Father, too. The entire Trinity is The Life. Therefore, the Holy Spirit was sent to be more than just the helper to remind us of Jesus' teachings, clarify His wisdom and help direct our lives. He was to be the Way to bring us into the eternal relationship with the entire Holy Trinity. In fact, the Holy Spirit is the only Way for us to be incorporated into our Creator's spiritual body and participate in the Life of God. Without believing in the resurrection of Jesus and making Him our Lord and Savior, Jesus would not send His Holy Spirit to us. Therefore, when Jesus proclaimed that, He "is the way, the truth, and the life; no one comes to the Father but through me" He was not boasting. He was just stating a fact. Without accepting Christ as his Lord and Savior, man would never receive the gift of the Holy Spirit, and without Him, man could never be reconnected with his Heavenly Father.

I used to think that the Holy Spirit was like a pinch of divine dough needed to make us into another loaf of godly bread. Now I believe the Holy Spirit is God's way of including us in the only relationship that would ever truly exist. **After we caterpillar "cancer cells" accepted Christ as our new God, He made us into a new creation, a butterfly that was no longer malignant. He also sent us the gift of the Holy Spirit, so we could be integrated into the person of God.** First, we had to respond to God's call and accept Him as our new God, so we could develop obedience to His will out of a deep love for Him. A human being's true life always starts with accepting God's love, and it becomes functional once God's love and character begins to flow through us.

Finally, as transformed cancer cells, our function is restored and we will be capable and willing to respond to the will of God,

our original Father cell. For cells to function well in His spiritual body, they must be able to respond to His direction quickly and exclusively. It is as if God wants to reprogram His human cancer cells to again live and operate under His authority. Then, He could literally give us our true purpose and designate our new role in the body of Christ. Jesus had to change our self-centered nature into a God-centered one, so we would take direction from the Father cell without question, thus allowing God to transmit His will and love through us. We are to be the cellular conduits through which God's desires and plans are transmitted, so He can accomplish His work on Earth and establish His Kingdom. As the Bible teaches, we become His hands and feet, but He is the one who directs our steps.

Since there is no room in Heaven for independent, rebellious caterpillars, there is no room in the body of Christ for cancer cells going off on a tangent and doing their own thing. **He wants to incorporate His lost children, His wayward, cancer cells into His eternal body, not merely incorporate His life into our mortal bodies.** He loves us so much; He wants us not only to live, but to have Life, His Life. True followers of Jesus are the church, which is more than a building or a congregation singing and praying together. It is virtually the "body of Christ." Nobody can have The Life without being in His body.

Just as individual cells die every day in our earthly body, cells die every day in the body of Christ. When human cells die, the spleen filters them out and sets them aside with no fanfare at all. However, when one of God's cells die, His Holy Spirit, which had permanently combined with His cell's spirit, carries both spirits home to a heavenly homecoming. God will greet him with those congratulatory words, "Well done, good and faithful servant!" (Matt. 25:23 NIV) For us butterflies, our homecoming will be like no *cell-ebration* you could ever imagine.

This perspective changes the way we interpret everything. Our new worldview; God's worldview, is born in us, and He reveals life's truths along the way. **When God has finished making us in His likeness, He incorporates us into His body and, as a result, we begin to know the mind of God. Remember, God does not learn. He knows. When we are transformed into God's likeness, we no longer learn God's wisdom. We know it.** Once our relationship with God is restored, God imparts His wisdom and truths to us. This is possible, because as interconnected cells in His body, God transmits to us whatever He wants us to know. He does not teach us His truths about our value to Him and our role in the world. We know these truths as a result of being part of Him. Because God is alive and always active, he can not stop doing His will to orient newly saved cells in His body. They must already have this information implanted in them, so they can quickly respond to His commands and carry out His will.

Living on Earth as breathing, thinking, learning, and pleasure seeking beings may be evidence that we are alive, but it is not The Life. **The natural, caterpillar way of human living is similar to a cancer cell that goes out on its own, living by itself, for itself, with no meaning and purpose greater than itself.** This way of living is merely a manifestation of a slow death before his final demise. Caterpillars may believe that existing outside the authority of God is true freedom, but it actually represents living like a prisoner on death row. They are nothing more than "dead men walking" experiencing transient happiness and pleasure interspersed within lives filled with fear, guilt, shame, pain, suffering and despair until they die.

Accepting Jesus as our Lord is the only *way* to replace The Liar with The Truth. Only when we respond to Christ's call and accept God's gift of His Son's sacrifice will the manufacturer, our Creator, cradle us while we die unto ourselves, then resurrect and restore His dysfunctional, malignant caterpillar cells. When we accept Christ as our Lord, He forgives our sins and washes us as white as snow. Then, God can declare us healthy and functional cells and accept us into His body, the body of Christ. Only then, can we become an active participant in God's spiritual body and experience the true life, His Life. Jesus is the only one who can offer us the cure for our malignant lives. He helps us make the leap from just existing until we die, to having and enjoying The Life, not just with God, but in God.

If we refuse God's call to be transformed by Jesus into butterflies, we can not receive His Spirit. Without His Spirit, we can not obtain God's Biblical worldview and the subsequent revelation and comprehension of His wisdom and truth. For in 1 Corinthians 2:14 (NLT) it says, "But people who are not spiritual can not receive these truths from God's spirit. It all sounds foolish to them, and they can not understand it, for only those who are spiritual can understand what the Spirit means." If we do not have God's Spirit in us, we can not adopt His view of life and can never truly make sense of the world into which we were born. If we choose to remain caterpillars, who live separated from God, we will never participate in the eternal love of Christ and will deny ourselves an eternal future with our Father in Heaven.

Once we realize that we can participate in the life of God, the notion of practicing any religion to earn God's favor so that He can merely participate as a servant in our lives is not only folly, it is an insult to God. When we settle for practicing a religion about God, we forfeit the opportunity to experience the true benefits of having a relationship with God. Religion is the product of man's self-centered nature. Unless his nature is transformed by Jesus, he will miss out on the chance of a lifetime to experience the fullness of living in and with God.

If we take my cancer-cell scenario to its logical conclusion, becoming a butterfly through the transforming power of Christ is the only psychological treatment and medical cure for the "cancer of human living." God makes us well by making us new, and He makes us new when we reinstate Him as our God and give Him final direction and authority over our lives. Unlike human treatments for cancer, the Great Physician cures our "cancer" by injecting His loving spirit into us rather than poisonous chemicals.

God's form of therapy is so much more sophisticated than ours. God only needs to wait for us to repent and spiritually die unto ourselves. After our spiritual rebirth, He transforms us from malignant beings into healthy new creations that are ready for a new life, our first life — His Life!

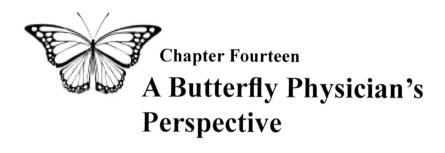

Chapter Fourteen
A Butterfly Physician's Perspective

But when Jesus heard this, He said, "It is not those who are healthy who need a physician, but those who are sick. But go and learn what this means, I desire compassion, and not sacrifice, for I did not come to call the righteous but sinners."

Matt. 9:12-13 (NASB)

"Let ... statesmen and patriots unite their endeavors to renovate the age by ... educating their little boys and girls ... and leading them in the study and practice of the exalted virtues of the Christian system."

Samuel Adams

I hope you enjoyed my caterpillar-butterfly illustration regarding abnormal and normal human psychology and behavior. I also hope you could see the truth of my analysis of American culture and the psychology of the self-centered, liberal and the God-centered, conservative worldviews. Finally, I hope that I have made it clear that Christianity is a worldview, not a weekend encounter with Catholicism or the Protestant religion of your personal, familial or cultural choice. **Being a Christian means becoming a follower of Jesus and living under His authority and control.** It involves much more than merely believing in Christ's existence and filling a church pew on an occasional Sunday. In fact, Christianity should not be confused with or compared to the practice of any of the world's religions, for Christianity is the antithesis of religion. It represents an intimate relationship with Christ, our Lord and Savior, who offers His followers a distinct psychological advantage in life. **Surrendering control of our lives to Christ and living under his authority is necessary for all human beings to achieve optimal mental health.** Only the Great Physician and the Wonderful Counselor can help man overcome his natural, dysfunctional state of mind.

I wrote this book as the "little physician," a Jewish man, a scientist, who has studied human behavior for over half of his life. I have practiced as a family physician and have treated tens of thousands of patients over three decades. During that time, I have gained a deep understanding of the human psyche and how it relates to God's wisdom and worldview. I have studied psychology, read philosophy and analyzed the Bible for many years. Yet, it was not until I decided to surrender my life to God by accepting Jesus as my Lord that I realized how dysfunctional my life had been. I could not learn to cure my dysfunctional behavior by reading the Bible or my medical books. In fact, I could not even see that my way of living was dysfunctional. I had to give up being my own boss before God would transform me and reveal the best way for me to live my life.

I spent the first forty years of my life as a wandering Jew in the spiritual desert of my own self-centered world. Fortunately for me, Christ continued to pursue me even after I rejected Him so many times before. My life as a heathen was extremely busy and full of accomplishments, but they were insufficient to overcome the personal discontentment, insecurity and fatigue I had been experiencing. I was suffering from being my own god, for he was a tough taskmaster, demanding that I worship him 24/7. No matter how hard I tried, I could never, once and for all, satisfy that overbearing god that looked just like me. After placing my faith in Jesus Christ, He rescued me from being my own god and the change in my attitude towards life was remarkable. I finally began to escape the world's gravitational pull towards self-involvement. In no time at all, my spirit lightened and my self-confidence increased considerably knowing how much God loved me.

God put my medical training and my predilection to overanalyze life to good use. After receiving Christ as my Lord and Savior, God gave me the spiritual gifts of encouragement and discernment. I believe God's gifts prompted me to use my over-analytical mind to discern the psychological truths revealed by Him in the Bible. The closer my relationship became with Jesus, the more fully He revealed His truth and wisdom to me. As my relationship with Him grew closer, He made it clear that the psychological health and quality of life for me and my fellow human beings depends upon whether we live under our own authority or God's. **Living under the authority of Christ is as necessary for optimal human living as blood is for maintaining life in the human body!**

My life's work now transcends the practice of medicine. It is to make the case for the truth that surrendering our lives to Christ, and living with Jesus as our God, is not now or ever has been a religious choice! **It is a medical necessity for the proper use and operation of the human body, the development of the healthiest psychological and emotional state of the human mind, and the highest spiritual development of the human heart.** If a person believes Christ is God, but does not surrender to His authority, he can never be transformed and restored. A true follower surrenders his autonomy to Christ, and once this occurs, he is capable of experiencing a more peaceful, rewarding and meaningful life.

Once we answer God's call to accept Jesus as our Lord and Savior, we can begin our therapeutic relationship with Him. This will allow us to receive the Great Physician's medical and psychological therapy, which will expose the lies that have poisoned our self-image since our childhood. The truth of God will transform our minds and heal our hearts in ways that will renew our lives forever.

The primary goal of my book is to engrave this next message in stone. **Developing a relationship with God is a medical decision, not a religious choice!** If people realize that surrendering to God's authority is necessary for sound mental and emotional health, then they will be able to transcend the traditional human barriers that have kept them from the healing hands of God. Allowing Christ to make more people brand new will substantially decrease the unnecessary misery and hopelessness that mankind has experienced for thousands of years.

Christ came to our world to become Our Savior. And, it is the doctor, not the priest, who saves lives. Jesus came to treat our past emotional injuries and address our spiritual emptiness and sinful behavior. Most people cringe at hearing the word *sin*. But, understanding its true meaning as it refers to medicine is extremely beneficial and is the key to understanding how God relates to us. Sin simply means dysfunction. Yes, sinful behavior reflects man's disobedience, and his disobedience may lead to poor decisions and outcomes. **However, the underlying truth is that sinful living is dysfunctional living.**

When God is not in control of the lives of His people, He views His creatures as sinful, dysfunctional, and incomplete. Incomplete people are handicapped people because they are missing something in the development of their bodies or brains, which compels them to operate and live in a dysfunctional manner. Just as nobody hates the handicapped, God does not hate us sinners, either. He may hate our decisions or our behavior because it hurts us and others, but he does not hate us. He is our Heavenly Father, and just like our human parents, He does not punish us every time we fall while learning to walk. God picks us up, dusts us off and encourages us to try again. He never gets so frustrated with human failure that He stops pursuing the lost or helping the found. He knew we were born in sin and were condemned at birth to live sinful, dysfunctional lives. He knew that if we did not have His Holy Spirit within us to guide us, we would stumble and fall and get lost in life. He would have to transform us before we could know His desired purpose for our lives, for we could never learn it on our own. Without the help of the Holy Spirit, it would be impossible to reach the heavenly destination Christ prepared for us over two thousand years ago.

God knew that if He did not personally come to complete His caterpillar people, they would certainly die in their sinful state. God may judge man's behavior as wrong-headed, reckless, or disobedient, but He does not deem His people, for whom He sacrificed His Son, as unacceptable or worthless. Therefore, God is able to hate the sin and love the sinner, and no sin is too big for Him to forgive. This does not mean God is not judgmental. He has to judge all people, for it is His righteous nature as a Holy God. But, He is also equally loving, which is why He sent Jesus to forgive our sin debt and redeem us. If we accept the sacrifice Jesus made on our behalf, He will make us clean and acceptable to live with our Father forever.

Until a caterpillar submits to God first, he can never know that his true and final form is to be a butterfly. The truth is only revealed to him by virtue of seeing himself transformed by the loving hands of God into a butterfly. **God does not need to explain the result of his handiwork to us. We *are* the result!** The surprising truth is that our value is equal to God's value because He redeemed us with His own life. Jesus bought us back and freed us from being a slave to our evil masters, ourselves. Consequently, He released us from being a slave to our neighbors' opinion and approval regarding our significance. It was not God's Word that set us free. It was Jesus on the cross that did so. Jesus is the Truth, and as He promised, The Truth shall set us free. Not until He lives within us, can we possibly know the Way in which we are to relate to God and our neighbors, and discover how to live the short, but abundant life God had planned for His butterflies.

Christ did not come to mend our broken hearts like a seamstress. He came as the Great Physician to resuscitate us after breaking us down, like the caterpillar structures in the cocoon, so He could perform a heart transplant and give us a new nature. He created our bodies in the Garden, but he was not finished with the final "renewing of our minds." God did not expect us to be separated from Him for our entire lives and die as dysfunctional caterpillars. He made us in his image, but His ultimate goal was to make our character into the likeness of His Son, Jesus. He has never been satisfied with merely making His primal and immature caterpillar people more functional by demanding that they behave better in spite of their congenital flaws and selfish nature. He is searching for surrendered caterpillars, who wanted to become butterflies by having Jesus replace them as the lord of their lives. He wanted us to set aside our old heart, our old nature, to make room for His transplanted heart. Once His perfect nature replaced our evil one, truly selfless, healthy behavior would occur more naturally and frequently.

Now we are born-again, truly alive, knowing the truth that we are not the lord of our lives! This time, we will no longer remain lost to God, wandering aimlessly in our self-centered world. This time, we will know that our lives belong to Jesus, and we are to follow Him and Him alone. This time, we will be filled with love for ourselves and our neighbors. This time, we will be able to experience the indescribable joy of serving our God and our fellow man. This time, when we live under Christ's authority, life will become a daily adventure. This time, we will live for eternal rewards rather than worldly ones, and we will experience the peace that surpasses all human understanding. Finally, we will truly know that our eternal souls are under the constant protection of God Almighty and our spirit will never again be separated from Him. Only when we dedicate our lives to pleasing God, who sent us a Savior to rescue us from death, does God's plan for our lives finally make sense to us.

God knows that it is not what we know, but who we know that makes life worth living. Therefore, we must know God in order to function as God designed. Once we know Him, we need to depend on Him to counsel us because we function best when He is in control. God knows we will flounder through life and remain lost forever if we insist on living according to our plans. In fact, God made this perfectly clear when He said, "For I know the plans I have for you," declares the Lord, "plans to prosper you and not to harm you, plans to give you hope and a future. (Jer. 29:11 NIV)

Only a caterpillar thinks that his plan for life is better than the one God planned specifically for him. In fact, if you want to make God laugh, tell him your plans.

When we live our way rather than His way, we will continue to live as caterpillars and condemn ourselves to the limited perspective and hellish life of self-centered larvae. What caterpillars do not realize is that God knew their purpose in life before they were born. They had no clue. God knew that serving others would give them their best feeling in life. They thought that getting others to serve them would give them their best feeling in life. God freely offered them His love. They thought they had to spend a lifetime earning it. From God's perspective, if they never relinquish control of their lives to Jesus, they will never understand His ways and know His divine truths. Acquiring the truth about our lives does not come from a college education, studying psychology or even reading the Bible. **Truth can only be known through a transformative relationship with Jesus Christ!**

Caterpillar people will suffer from mental and psychological dysfunction each day they stubbornly continue to live under their own authority. If they reach the end of their lives without accepting God's gift of transformation, they will forever be condemned to do what caterpillars loved doing most while on Earth, which was munching leaves (serving themselves) and crawling over or around others (ignoring or harming their neighbors). The true life that God offers them can only be lived as a butterfly equipped with wings that will add grace and beauty to each other's gardens and allow them to ascend to Heaven when they pass away. Individually and collectively, if caterpillar people refuse God's transformation, there will be hell to pay. Unfortunately, things literally will get too hot for them before they realize that it is too late to receive God's gift of butterfly wings needed to escape the eternal fires in hell.

The Bible proclaims that people who die without knowing Him are condemned to eternal separation from Him. Therefore, eternal separation from God is death; living as a caterpillar is death; a self-centered life is death. People can not live their lives with the same perspective and self-centered nature they had when they were born and expect to experience an earthly and eternal life with God. Only when God transplants His heart in them and they are born again, can they ever have the spark of God's Spirit in them and truly know God.

The caterpillars, who remain stubborn will regret their choice to ignore God's call to become butterflies. Unfortunately, they will have plenty of time to reflect on their decision while dwelling in the darkness and scorching heat of the lake of fire for eternity with the billions of other rebellious and defiant caterpillars. In between wailing and gnashing of teeth, they will plead with God to make them quickly and magically into butterflies, so they can fly away and escape their endless, tormenting existence. Sadly, for every newly admitted caterpillar, God's life-long offer to become a butterfly had expired the day before. Now that's Hell!

This is an opportune time to clear up a common misconception regarding the death of our friends and loved ones. God knows from the beginning of time when each of us will die and in what manner. Consequently, God does not take the lives of our loved ones as I have heard so many people say. God merely accepts or rejects them after they die based on whether His Son Jesus says He knows them or not. Since Jesus was intimately involved in the transformation and lives of His butterflies, He has previous knowledge of them and accepts them into Heaven. Since caterpillars have chosen not to know Him, He rejects them. God just separates the wheat from the chaff. Simple, as that!

Christ's Goal: Niceness or Peace?

In the past thirty years, I have treated tens of thousands of patients and the vast majority of them were truly nice people. In fact, the world is filled with nice people. I have encountered nice atheists, Christians, Muslims, Jews, Buddhists and Hindus. Since nice people are found among all religious and non-religious people, then niceness must be a function of being human, not a special characteristic or product of religion or non-religion. Niceness is universal.

Unfortunately, since bad things happen in our world and no person is nice all of the time, these same nice people, who exhibit neighborly and generous behavior one day, may exhibit destructive and evil behavior the next. Since evil is found among religious and non-religious people, evil must be a result of being human, not a special characteristic of religion or non-religion. Evil is universal.

If the practice of religion was to deter nice people from committing evil, or turn evil people into nice people, then religion failed miserably. Even the perfect life and sacrificial death of Jesus has not made the world a more congenial and less dangerous place. It is still a cauldron boiling over with injustice and evil. Did Christ fail in his mission to make man nice? Or, was making man nice and the world a nicer place, not Our Savior's primary goal?

God is perfect! He never fails to fulfill his will. If niceness was His goal, then the world would be a nice place. Niceness, also called kindness, is a personality trait that is either cultivated or corrupted by our upbringing or our culture. Good deeds are performed by nice people out of love for their neighbor, or by evil-doers for self-centered reasons intended to benefit themselves. Good deeds are viewed by people as righteous. However, in Isaiah, 64:6 (NIV), the message is, when man's good deeds are compared to God's righteousness, man's good deeds "are like filthy rags" before Him. Christ did not sacrifice His life so that we could do more good deeds than evil ones. If God's true goal is to make man in His likeness, then merely making man less evil would be an abject failure. God came to our world to offer human beings a chance to obtain something more impactful and life-changing. He did not come here merely to improve man's demeanor.

213

Jesus taught that the gates to Heaven are narrow. He knew that all men would not accept his forgiveness, mercy and grace and be transformed into His likeness. Consequently, our world would remain filled with self-indulgent and evil people. Christ's mission was to transform willing people into butterflies, who would become His new brothers and sisters. Jesus knew that if the world hated Him, it would surely hate his new family members, as well. Yet, Jesus commands all of his butterflies to do His will, which includes spreading the Gospel in a cruel, unpredictable and dangerous world. Making us into nicer people, who do more good works, may help improve our world. However, niceness alone would not help His new-born family members cope with the hardship and emotional stress of living the remainder of their lives in an unfair and tumultuous world. Jesus needed to bestow upon his new family members a gift that would be vastly more helpful to them. God would not command us to spread the Gospel in a hostile world without providing us with emotional and psychological relief from the hardship and stress of following His commands.

The answer is clearly stated in the story of Christ's birth, yet most Christians, including myself, missed it. God's reasons for coming to Earth are found in Luke 2:14. God sent a host of angels to proclaim, "Glory to God in the highest heaven, and on earth peace to those on whom his favor rests." **We were to proclaim God's glory to the world. However, God knew we would need to have peaceful hearts and minds to persevere and be successful.** Only butterflies, who participate in the Great Commission to make disciples of all nations, receive God's gift of emotional and spiritual peace. Nice caterpillars, who occasionally do good deeds, will find neither peace nor rest as a result of their *good* behavior.

Practitioners of all religions have a general sense that it is better to have God's peace than not, but because of their human, self-centered nature, they automatically assume they must find a way to earn peace. The angels did not declare that peace comes to those who earn it. They only said man will have peace if God places his favor on Him. **Peace is God's to give, not man's to earn.** Yes, man must do something for God to grant him peace, but He can not earn it. Peace comes through surrendering our autonomy to God, not performing good works. In order for religious or non-religious people to experience emotional and psychological peace, they need to see themselves as caterpillars needing to be transformed into butterflies, for only butterflies can experience God's peace and live more functional lives.

How Should We View the Bible?

God has made His Truth available to people through His Word, The Bible. His wisdom becomes knowable to butterflies through their relationship with Jesus, but caterpillars can not fully understand the decrees, laws and commandments written in it by their Creator because they have not yet surrendered the authority of their lives to God. The Bible does not make the Christian, God does. Until God's caterpillars accept that God is God, and they are not, all the wisdom in the Holy Bible can not make caterpillar men into butterflies acceptable to God.

Since human beings accumulate medical knowledge in bits and pieces, libraries are bursting at the seams with millions of obsolete science and medical books written throughout the ages by learned doctors and revered scientists. In fact, I have heard the Louvre in Paris houses three and a half miles of shelves full of them. Remarkably, the Bible has outlived them all. **It will never become obsolete because regardless of the level of our understanding regarding the cellular and chemical operation of the human mind and body, the optimal perspective from which we live that life will never change.** God knew that man could experience a peaceful and meaningful life with Him, even though he may have little understanding about the operation and function of his own complex mind and body. God also knew that man would live a dysfunctional, turbulent and miserable life without Him, regardless how sophisticated his understanding was regarding the operation and function of his own mind and body.

Therefore, advances in medicine and science can not guarantee an individual's peaceful spirit and healthy psyche. Without God at the controls guiding men's steps, their paths through life will be chaotic and tortuous, and they will get lost and stay lost. Not only will they never reach the place God intended for them to spend eternity, they will eventually hurt or destroy themselves and harm those closest to them. No matter how advanced medicine becomes, it will never become sophisticated enough to make a prosthetic that will replace God as our internal guidance system. **The "created" can never create the Creator.** We human doctors can never make our patients totally well unless they are made entirely whole by God. So, we must refer them back to the manufacturer for completion. No matter how advanced medicine becomes, doctors will never be able to transform a caterpillar into a butterfly. Only God can do that!

Since caterpillar people believe they should have the final word over God, they assume they have the authority to select passages from of the Bible that suit them. They view the Bible as a religious book; a compilation of man's ancient writings that contain nuggets of man's wisdom that might help them live their lives.

What if they viewed the Bible as a medical book instead of a religious one? How would their attitude towards the Bible change, if they viewed the Bible as a medical book that provided a detailed therapeutic plan designed to address and treat their evil nature and cure the *cancer of human living*? My guess is that they would be much less likely to skip even one passage if they believed they would suffer complications, treatment failure or death.

Since religion is not from God, the Bible was not intended to be a religious book. It was the Great Physician's Medical Manual inspired by Our Creator, Himself. **The Bible is to serve as man's comprehensive medical textbook and psychological primer describing the proper way for man to live his life, and more importantly, for whom to**

live his life. It is obvious that the manufacturer should be the one to write the Owner's Manual.

My medical books explain how life operates within my body, but the Bible describes the manner in which the human organism is to live that life. As a physician, I studied my medical textbooks to learn medical and surgical treatments that would help my patients recover from illness and be restored to, at least, a reasonable level of health. The Bible, however, shows us how the Great Physician transforms us from dead caterpillars walking into live butterflies flying through life into eternity. The treatment for man's dysfunctional life is to live under God's control, but we can only receive His treatment by asking Jesus to come into our hearts as the new God of our lives.

In fact, so much of the wisdom of the Bible can not be obtained by just opening the cover and reading it. Our ability to understand and implement Biblical teaching can only occur with the guidance and clarification of the Holy Spirit, which allows us to read it from God's perspective. It is as if we need special glasses in order to read His Word through His eyes. This is the only way to understand the true meaning of His wisdom and experience the beneficial effects of His advice.

Merely reading His instruction manual will be an inadequate substitute for a transforming relationship with God. The ancient Jews tried that with the Torah and fell short of God's expectation. We must submit to Christ's authority and become His followers in order to understand the truth of His Word. When Jesus proclaimed He was "the Truth," He meant that nothing would ever make sense to us unless He personally revealed the truth to us. However, He will not reveal the truth to a stranger who has no interest in developing a relationship with Him.

The Bible functions as God's Owner's Manual, and the critical message in His manual is that *we* are not the owners! If we do not accept this fact, it will be impossible for us to understand and implement the instructions and wisdom in the Bible. Since we are not designed to be our own god, we can not function properly without living under God's authority. If we do not accept that God is the actual owner of our bodies and our lives, it will be impossible to develop the correct and functional worldview, and we will never find hope and peace with God.

Making Sense of the Garden of Eden and the Fall of Man

Contrary to popular belief, caterpillars may have thought they were their own boss, but they have really never been in control. They have been just as deceived as Eve was in the Garden when Satan enticed her into thinking that she could be like God, and mercilessly led her away from Him like a lamb to the slaughter. Sadly, Adam and Eve did not expect that their disobedience would cause them to be expelled from the Garden and their daily participation in The Life of God would abruptly end. Our Creator's ultimate desire for Adam and Eve was not to crawl right behind Satan, but for them to receive butterfly wings to soar above Satan's influence while on Earth and after their deaths return to Him in Heaven.

When Adam and Eve rebelled against God's authority, He was not surprised because He is omniscient. God can see the future and the present at the same time. Therefore, He witnesses our sinful behavior before it happens. Since our sinful behavior can never be a surprise to Him, it is impossible for us to disappoint God. When it comes to the fall of man, God already knew that Satan would deceive Adam and Eve. They would eventually be seduced away from His authority. God knew that when they disobeyed Eden's only rule, they would be expelled from Eden and Satan would be free to influence them.

Satan's job was simple. All he had to do was prevent the metamorphosis of his earthly caterpillars into butterflies. Without this transformation, they would not have the wings to escape the fallen world's gravitational hold on them and return to their real

Father in Heaven. In order to accomplish this, he needed to keep them separated from God. As long as Satan was successful in this singular task, Adam and Eve and all of their caterpillar descendants would remain caterpillars condemned to follow the serpent's path away from God.

The essence of Satan's nature was self-centeredness, which is why God banished him from Heaven in the first place. He fooled Adam and Eve into joining him in a life separated from God, thus condemning them to scratch out an existence from the earth. Satan wanted to influence them into imitating his own self-centered, sinful nature because he knew that their self-centeredness would inevitably keep them separated from God, resulting in their permanent deaths. Before Satan could deceive Adam and Eve, he had to mislead them regarding the truth of God's nature. Satan had to convince them that serving themselves and becoming their own bosses were the prerequisites to becoming like God. The truth, of course, is just the opposite. God's true nature is to be a servant until death as Jesus demonstrated by His crucifixion. Once Adam and Eve accepted this lie about the nature of God, it was easy for Satan to deceive them into believing that satisfying their own urges and fulfilling their own will was all it took to be like God. Satan made them think they were going to live like gods, when he actually condemned them to live like slaves.

All human beings are Adam and Eve's progeny, so our innate self-image as the god of our lives is more than theological, it is biological. We are congenitally programmed to see ourselves to be like god and be in control of our lives. Consider a human baby. His parents feed him, warm him, change him, bathe him, play with him, protect him and they are there for him almost every time he cries. Although the baby's parents provide him with everything and serve him day in and day out, does the newborn see his parents, his providers as God? Of course, not! From his immature, larval perspective, he sees that life is about getting his urges, needs, and desires fulfilled. He sees himself as the one in control, and he comes to the natural, but erroneous, conclusion that he is the focus of his existence. **The self-centered nature of man was formed and revealed at the same time. The dysfunctional life of a human begins at birth.**

Written in the Book of Genesis, God had a plan for man's rescue and salvation prior to Adam and Eve's fall from grace. He was to arrive in the form of Jesus (God) to live among us, die on the cross, and be resurrected. God, our Creator and our manufacturer, had to return in person to perform His transformative and restorative work on His caterpillars. Since God created all living things, He knew that butterflies could only come from caterpillars. Therefore, in order to fulfill His plan for his human creatures to become butterflies, He needed them to experience the world from a caterpillar's perspective. God knew what He was doing. He knew from the beginning of time that He could turn what Satan intended for evil, "into good for those who love God and are called according to His purpose." (Romans 8:28 NIV)

Darwinism and the Decline of America

Until 1859, when Darwin published *The Origin of Species*, most Americans accepted living under God's authority and considered it a normal and natural state of being. Although the theory of evolution was never proved, caterpillars all over the world assumed it to be true. To America's detriment, the acceptance of the theory of evolution, as truth, turned out to be the beginning of the end of our colonial fathers' dream for a God-centered America. Once people accepted Darwinism above the hand of God as an explanation for the origin of life, they began to perceive God as irrelevant and rejected His authority over their lives. In time, people chose to worship the philosophy of evolution espoused by scientists instead of the infallible Word of God.

Many have referred to the theory of evolution as the "law of evolution" for so long, human beings have accepted it as fact.

According to Darwin, if only one piece of evidence were found to be inconsistent or contrary to his theory, evolution as a reasonable explanation for the origin of life would fall apart. Over the decades, we have discovered mathematical, physical, genetic, biochemical, archeological, cosmological and anthropological evidence, which could discredit the theory of evolution as an explanation for the origin of life. If today's scientists were honest with themselves, they would concede that the theory of evolution fails to hold water. However, these stubborn scientists are also caterpillars, and as caterpillars, they would rather exchange the truth for a lie in order to maintain their god-like status and remain unaccountable to God for their behavior.

We humans should have known better than to worship science as our new god, because through the ages, the scientific community has misled us into believing faulty science. Remember, before Copernicus, the scientific community convinced our ancestors that the Sun revolved around the Earth and the Earth was flat. I can remember, as recently as thirty years ago, that antihypertensive drugs called beta-blockers were contraindicated in congestive heart failure. Today, we may be sued if our patients with heart failure have not been prescribed beta-blockers. It is clear that human scientists have been wrong many times regarding the operation of our bodies and our natural world. Evolutionary theory is just another example. We need to expose the fallacy of macro-evolution, and toss it into the trash heap of history with the rest of man's erroneous scientific theories.

Over the course of a century and a half, our acceptance of evolution as fact has caused much of American society to lose its healthy God-centered perspective of life. As more and more of our citizens dismissed God as the central figure of their existence, America became more self-indulgent and began her slow decline into mediocrity. As more Americans chose to live as if they were no longer accountable to God, the moral fabric of our society began to unravel.

Fortunately, I believe that there is still enough of our founders' cloth remaining to restore God's blanket of salvation and protection for America, *if* we regain control over our education system and Christian researchers help keep the scientific and medical community honest. True science involves considering all the possible variables to a problem. Evolutionary scientists eliminated God and Creation as a possible explanation for the origin of life before they began their investigation and research to verify the theory of evolution. We need members of these three institutions to assist our pastors in refuting evolution, and help educate our patients on the healthiest worldview from which to live their lives.

The scientific community needs to do more to improve our patients' lives than merely extending their lives. Physicians and other health care providers need to inform our patients of the mental and physical benefits of seeking a relationship with Jesus. Why strive to develop more sophisticated medical treatments and technology that will increase our patients' longevity, if we are not willing to help them find more peace and joy in the process? Helping our patients develop a relationship with Christ will allow them to live the healthiest and most rewarding lives possible.

Chapter Fifteen

The Little Physician's Prescription for a New Life

The man without the Spirit does not accept the things that come from the Spirit of God, for they are foolishness to him, and he cannot understand them, because they are spiritually discerned.

1 Corinthians 2:14 NIV

Without a humble imitation of the characteristics of the Divine Author of our blessed religion, we can never hope to be a happy nation."

George Washington

When I was a caterpillar, life was constantly about fulfilling my will and executing my plans. I achieved everything I ever dreamed of and more, yet I still felt empty and insecure. My family and friends considered me successful, but I was not a happy camper, especially in my marriage, which ended in a horribly painful divorce. I grew up like any other caterpillar, thinking my worth was based on my achievements and my performance, which led me to believe I was worthless every time I made a mistake. Life to me was about being perfect. It caused me to fear failure to such an extent, I was hesitant to venture out and expand my horizons. I needed to feel worthy and lovable in spite of my failings and my lack of confidence. I was not living life correctly, and I needed guidance from someone who was much smarter than me. Jesus came to my rescue and loved me when I was having difficulty loving myself. He could separate

223

my behavior and performance from my true value. Through His forgiveness and affirmation, He set me free to live with much less self-condemnation every time I made a mistake.

To my disappointment, merely being baptized and going to church did not magically heal me. I had accepted Jesus as my Savior, and my belief in Him was genuine. However, my profession of faith in Jesus Christ as my God was incomplete. Accepting Him as my Savior, but not my Lord, was not enough to change my impression of myself and correct my worldview. Before Jesus transformed me into a new person, I had to offer my life as a sacrifice and make Him my Lord. This was not an easy task for me. As a physician, I spent all day being in control of my practice, so giving control of my life to God was a totally new concept for me. **I had to place myself at the foot of the cross every day, and sometimes many times per day, because I kept crawling off to resume control of my life.** When I perform a procedure or render a treatment, my patients must lie on the exam table and give me control of their bodies for a few minutes. Similarly, I had to lie totally helpless and vulnerable on the altar before God, the Great Physician, so He could perform my much needed heart transplant. After He completed His spiritual surgery, my values and priorities changed. In no time at all, my belief in my own intrinsic worth flourished.

Now I see myself as a butterfly, but I am still working on becoming more dependent upon God. The closer my relationship with Jesus becomes, the more I can feel His love and the more clearly I can see my true self reflected in His eyes. When I was a caterpillar and read the Bible, it represented nothing more to me than mundane history and fairy tales. Now, as a butterfly, I can read the Bible and its meaning regarding how to love and live my life is perfectly clear. Now, God's worldview makes total sense to me.

My self-centered nature rears its ugly head at times when I feel stressed. But, I am learning to recover more quickly by reassuring myself that regardless of the situation I find myself, God will control that situation to strengthen my character. As it says in Romans 5:3-4 (NIV), "... but we also glory in our sufferings, because we know that suffering produces perseverance; perseverance, character; and character, hope." I am totally confident that He will use my temporary emotional pain and confusion to make me more resilient, more forgiving, and more loving. I am not a fully mature butterfly yet, but since I have accepted Jesus Christ as my Lord *and* Savior, I have stopped making dysfunctional living a career!

As I mentioned earlier, my mother was Jewish and, like many Jewish mothers, she expressed the hope of her son becoming a doctor even before my birth. She even named me David James because she thought "D.J. Delnostro, M.D." would look professional on a shingle. I worked hard in school to make my Jewish mother's dream come true, but I grew up with little or no religious upbringing except for attending Hebrew school for two years when I was ten or eleven. The reason I bring up my Jewish heritage is that my belief in Christ was not a product of being raised in a Christian family. I accepted Jesus when I was a physician, not out of desperation, but out of feelings of emptiness. As a physician, I understood the benefit of healing relationships, so entering into a relationship with God made perfect sense to me on a medical and psychological level.

I learned from my medical practice that the vast majority of human emotional pain results from dysfunctional and broken relationships. So, it seemed logical to me that healing must also come through a therapeutic relationship with a doctor or a therapist. In order to heal my unsettled psyche and listless spirit, I needed to be under the care of an exceptionally spiritual physician. There was no one more qualified to cure what ailed me than the Great Physician. Jesus accepted me as His patient, and He never gave up on me. When I finally submitted myself to God through Christ, He established my value and showered me with love, which human counselors are unable to do because they need to preserve their objectivity. When I wholeheartedly accepted Christ's sacrifice on the cross, He invited me into a new relationship with God and this relationship became my treatment. **God did not teach me how much He loved and valued me. He showed me by sacrificing His Son on the cross! He did not explain to me how special I was to Him. He remade me in His likeness! He did not adopt me into His family. He allowed me to be reborn as His child! Not only did my Heavenly Father immaculately conceive me in His spiritual cocoon. His Son delivered me!**

My Prescription for My Fellow Physicians

Imagine if people saw the Bible as a medical book and Jesus as a doctor rather than a religious leader. They might follow Jesus as part of their medical treatment rather than viewing Him as a mythical or historical religious figure who magically intervenes to repair or rebuild their lives. To paraphrase Dr. David Jeremiah from one of his sermons on The Book of Revelation, he said the goal of reading the Bible is not as much for man to learn to interpret the Bible, but to have the God of the Bible interpret man. Not only is the truth about God evident in this Holy Book, but the truth about our value to God and His love for us also becomes clear.

In the Bible, which is the Great Physician's Medical Manual, He offers to heal us through a direct relationship with Him. It is within this divine relationship that man's sinful nature begins to be countered by God's selfless nature. His universal prescription for healing the emotional and psychological damage from man's dysfunctional and self-destructive behavior is not by rendering a treatment. His involvement in our lives *is* the treatment. He does not waste time offering us therapy by delving into our past. He forgives us our past through his grace and mercy, and He heals us by making us into new creations. New creations do not have a past that can continue to haunt them and adversely affect them for the rest of their lives. Once they place their trust in God, their perspective will change, which will allow them to heal psychologically and emotionally. This healing of the psyche will free them from past guilt and shame. Having a clean conscience before God will allow them to better obey God's commandments and instructions written in the Owner's Manual.

When people turn over control of their lives to Christ, their self-centered worldview diminishes, and they will be able to see God as their helper, not their warden or cosmic killjoy. Now, they can freely call on Him, and through His counsel, He will minister to their spiritual and emotional needs. Unlike human physicians, God can offer forgiveness, grace, mercy, love and rebirth to our patients. The best we "little physicians" can do is to repair their physical injuries and mask or numb their physical and emotional pain with medication. We can help them just enough to keep them alive so that they can crawl through life like a caterpillar, whose skin is so scarred from his past traumas, he can hardly feel the joy God had intended for him. Therefore, if we truly want the best for our patients, we must never withhold the Gospel from them. We must realize that no matter how proficient we physicians become in healing and restoring our patients, the death rate in our practices will never fall below 100%. Therefore, why would we ever hesitate to introduce them to the Great Physician, who can fully heal their hearts and minds and give them a new life that will last for eternity?

The message to my fellow physicians and the world at large is that human beings live better lives if they possess a God-centered, Biblical worldview, and they live their best lives if they make Christ their Lord and live under His authority. The ultimate goal of all physicians should be to help their caterpillar patients' metamorphosis into butterflies because butterflies are more psychologically and emotionally grounded. They have more stable and healthy relationships, and they engage in fewer risky and destructive behaviors that might result in physical and emotional harm. From a physician's perspective, encouraging people to live according to God's Biblical worldview should be included as a part of every patient's medical and psychological health care plan. It will address and improve their emotional, psychological and self-worth issues that spawn all sorts of human unhappiness and pathological behavior. Once our patients begin living under the care of the Great Physician and the Wonderful Counselor, our chance of helping them achieve healthy and successful medical outcomes will increase significantly.

The simple truth is that living life from God's perspective is necessary to achieve optimal mental and physical health. I believe that studying the Gospel and the Biblical worldview should be a mandatory part of a physician's education and should be offered in every medical school. Physicians, who are followers of Christ, should share the Gospel with their patients and encourage the acceptance of Christ as Lord and Savior. What is the benefit of achieving medical advances that will prolong our patients' lives, if we physicians are not going to refer them to the Great Physician, who prescribed the healthiest, most rewarding way to live that life? Once leading people to Christ is sanctioned as part of our medical training and is accepted as part of our patient's medical treatment, what could be easier for a doctor to do than to make the referral to The Great Physician? Can you imagine? No objection on religious grounds, for Christianity is not a religion, but a worldview! No arguing with insurance companies! No appointment necessary! No paperwork! No co-pay for our patients! It is as if we have gone to Heaven. And, if we make the referral, maybe more of our patients will go, as well.

The health of our country depends on the mental health and emotional stability of each American, and the level of their mental health status depends on living according to a God-centered, Biblical worldview. Living as one nation under God was the way our forefathers saw the world when they conceived and birthed America. It was the Judeo-Christian, Biblical worldview that allowed America to evolve into the greatest country the world has ever known. It was our faith in Jesus and our acceptance that God was in control that gave America her unique worldview and moral standing in the world. This Biblical perspective was the key to America becoming the civilized world's greatest purveyor of generosity and good will. Reviving the Gospel and evangelizing America is the only way to guarantee our country's return to health and her former greatness. America looks to us, the best trained physicians in the world, to make her healthy again. We can not merely offer them medical treatments without the counsel and love of God and expect this healing to occur.

Prevention is the medical and scientific byword of our day. We recommend wearing seatbelts while driving and helmets while riding bikes to protect our heads. Yet, we allow the godless philosophy of evolution, disguised as science, to be taught in our schools to permeate and poison the minds of our youth against the reality of God. Physicians recommend restricting access to cigarettes, drugs, alcohol, and guns, yet we do nothing to address the evil nature of man that drives him into misusing and abusing these things. The medical establishment in government warns our patients of the harmful effects of sugary soft drinks and fatty, salt-laden foods. They spend millions on government campaigns to promote regular exercise. Yet, these same Liberals, who want to regulate and control our patients' unhealthy behaviors, have worked diligently to remove God from public view, thus preventing our people from accepting that caring for our bodies is a means of worshipping the God that made them. We know the harm pornography and unprotected sex does to our patients, but we will not address our patient's dysfunctional caterpillar nature that drives them into these self-abusive and destructive behaviors. Society relentlessly campaigns against obesity and smoking because diabetes and heart disease takes years off of our lives. Yet, at the same time, they promote the acceptance of the homosexual lifestyle as healthy and normal, knowing that a 20 year old gay man's lifespan is 8-20 years shorter than the lives of all men.

If we truly wanted to make an impact on the health of our neighbors, it would be more appropriate for the medical community and society to encourage our patients to seek and worship Jesus. Then, He could give them a new nature and the proper worldview necessary to fight against these unhealthy urges and desires. It seems implausible to me that by merely encouraging our caterpillar patients to defy their own self-centered nature and use their limited willpower to control their unhealthy and pathological behaviors, we will ever make a significant difference in their lives.

My Prescription for All of God's Caterpillars

I believe God has given me the gift of discernment and the Holy Spirit has made it possible for me to know a portion of His wisdom. He is allowing me to participate in The Great Commission by guiding me through this psychological dissertation on the God-centered, Biblical and the self-centered, non-Biblical worldviews. My prescription for all of God's caterpillars is expressed in a prayer for their transformation into God's beloved butterflies.

Dear Heavenly Father,

I pray that all who read this work of love will be convinced that Jesus is the Truth and accept Him as their Lord and Savior. I lift up my wingless caterpillar brothers and sisters to you, Lord, and pray they stop living as their own individual gods and surrender their will to yours, so you can save them from their meaningless and hopeless caterpillar lives. Transform them into butterflies that can fully understand your wisdom and follow your instructions in the Bible regarding the best way to live their lives. Transplant in them your servant's heart and reveal to them your deep and endless love. Give them wings so that they can see the truth of the world from your perspective. Most of all, Lord, I pray that all of your caterpillars will surrender their lives into the transforming hands of Christ, who will bestow on them the butterfly wings necessary to ascend to their true and perfect home in Heaven! It is in your Son's name I pray.

Amen.

I have taken some artistic liberty with God's most liberating message in the Bible, John 3:16, "God so loved *His caterpillar people* that whosoever believes in Him would not perish, but have everlasting life *as His butterfly children*."

My prescription for all of God's dysfunctional, handicapped caterpillars, who are suffering from man's congenital self-centered nature, is not to patch you up and send you to the front line of life unprepared and unarmed. My job, as the little physician, is to bind your wounds while God heals them and refer you to *the* specialist, the Great Physician, who is skilled enough to do what I can not... transform you into a butterfly. I hope you will fill my prescription today. Don't worry about the cost because Jesus already paid for it on the cross over two thousand years ago. To be truthful, Christ will not administer His divine medicine. He is the medicine! And, when God is the medicine, just one dose will last forever and ever!

Praise and glory to my Lord and Savior, Jesus Christ!

It is time to begin your butterfly life!

Epilogue:
My Prescription for America

My prescription to revive and restore America is for more American caterpillars to ask Jesus to transform them into butterflies. I designed my book to remove the intellectual obstacles that prevent Americans from turning to God. It should be no surprise that my plan, based on a logical psychological analysis, is consistent with God's wisdom and truth found in the Bible.

1. My contention is that every human being worships a god from birth, and there is no such thing as an atheist. The God of our lives is the one upon whom we center our lives and who's will we aspire to fulfill. We are either "caterpillars" that worship ourselves as god or "butterflies" that worship God through Christ. These are the only two worldviews available to mankind. As far as my country is concerned, America can only hope to soar again, if caterpillars are transformed into butterflies

2. Publicly disprove Evolution as the origin of human life, which will remove the greatest intellectual obstacle that prevents people from turning to God. I doubt if there is a cellular biologist, zoologist, chemist, physicist, archeologist, paleontologist, or mathematician who has reviewed the current scientific data that can honestly claim the "evolutionary theory" explains the origin of life. Totally eliminating the notion that life could have sprung from "primordial goo" would compel people to see without a doubt that God's hand was involved in the creation of human life. There are so many arguments already available to disprove evolution as the origin of life, it is just a matter of finding the best way to teach our children and provide our neighbors with the truth.

3. Demonstrate how religions actually prevent us from a healing relationship with God. Many of our world religions can offer comfort to the afflicted and downtrodden, but merely following

a belief system in an attempt to earn God's favor to do our will, falls short of the therapeutic goal of transforming our self-centered evil nature. We can not begin to change the evil nature of our world unless we enlist Christ's help to counter the evil nature of the caterpillar people living in it.

4. Demonstrate and prove that Christianity is a worldview, not a religion. The acceptance of this truth will eliminate legal challenges regarding the promotion of Christianity and separation of "church and state" issues that has prevented the Christ-centered worldview to be publicly accepted and openly taught in the public schools.

5. Have the Bible reclassified as a medical book rather than a religious one, which would make it available for study again in our public schools, universities and medical schools. If the Bible is offered and accepted into the realm of behavioral science and psychology, as it should be, the teaching of the Biblical worldview will be deemed necessary for human beings to live functional and healthy lives.

Are you a caterpillar or butterfly?

God's Biblical Butterfly Worldview	Man's Caterpillar Worldview
God created the universe and man	Universe and man are products of evolution
God (Jesus) is God and sovereign	Man is god and sovereign
Man's life belongs to God; dependent	Man's life is his own; independent
Everything belongs to God including us	Everything we have belongs to us
Man is to serve God and other men	God serves man and man serves himself
Man is to please God	Man is to please himself
Man is to do God's will	God is to do Man's will
Man's role is to be a steward of the earth	Man can control and save the earth
Man is to love God	Man is to love the world
God is the truth, only one truth	All Truth is relative, many truths
Tolerance is to love others in spite of their different viewpoints	Tolerance means all viewpoints are equally valid and true
Man has an evil nature	Man is generally good
Man has a body and spirit	Man is only protoplasm

God's Biblical Butterfly Worldview	Man's Caterpillar Worldview
Heaven is for the forgiven and surrendered to Christ	Heaven, if it exists is for good people
God is actively involved in our lives	God may not exist, if he does, he is irrelevant
Perspective is God-centered	Perspective is self-centered
Man grows by transformation	Man grows through information
God determines man's significance	People determine man's significance
Human nature can be transformed	Human nature is genetic and fixed
Satan influences man's behavior on earth	Man is under no external control
Sin is anything done outside of God's will	Sin does not exist since there's no God
Belief in Jesus makes us right with God	Good works makes us right with God
Peace comes only when all worship one God, Jesus Christ	Peace achieved by correcting our behavior and controlling others
Bible is only instruction book on way to live	Individuals determines their way to live, many ways
We please God through having faith in Him	We please God by obeying His laws and commandments

God's Biblical Butterfly Worldview	Man's Caterpillar Worldview
God is in control, protection reduces fear	Man can't control future, fear abounds
God always loves man	Man occasionally loves his neighbor
God expects man to meet his responsibilities	Man is obsessed with his rights
God always answers prayers: yes, no, maybe, later	God answers prayers if we deserve it
God has authority over governments	God has no authority over government
God is our provider	Government is our provider
God's provision is a privilege to receive	Government owes us entitlements
God expects even the poor to tithe	The poor do not have to pay taxes
God offers His wisdom	Man turns to science and education
God fixes people	Man fixes problems
God looks to the future for man's healing	Man looks to the past for his healing
God is concerned with man's character	Man is concerned with his comfort
God works to change man's heart	Man tries to change his circumstances

Works Cited

Chapter 1
"Christian Quotes of the Founding Fathers." *About.com*. N.p., n.d. Web. Feb. 2011

Chapter 2
Henry, Patrick. "Patrick Henry Quotes." *Revolutionary War and Beyond*. N.p., n.d. Web. Mar. 2011

Rose Franklin. "Monarch Butterfly Metamorphosis." *Butterfly Bushes*. N.p., 2010. Web. May 2011.

Chapter 3
Webster, Daniel. "Land of the Free - A Conservative Politics Web Site." *The Land of the Free*. N.p., 2011. Web. Mar. 2011.

Chapter 4
Madison, James. "Land of the Free - A Conservative Politics Web Site." *The Land of the Free*. N.p., 2011. Web. Mar. 2011.

Chapter 5
Washington, George. "Land of the Free - A Conservative Politics Web Site." *The Land of the Free*. N.p., 2011. Web. Mar. 2011.

Lewis, C.S. *Mere Christianity*. Rev. ed. New York, NY: Macmillan Publishing Company, 1952. 109-114. Print.

Chapter 6
Hamilton, John Church. *History of the Republic of the United States of America: As Traced in the Writings of Alexander Hamilton and of His*. 7. Gale, Making of Modern Law, 2010. 790. Print.

Chapter 7
Webster, Noah. "Land of the Free - A Conservative Politics Web Site." *The Land of the Free*. N.p., 2011. Web. Mar. 2011.

Chapter 8
Franklin, Benjamin. "Land of the Free - A Conservative Politics Web Site." *The Land of the Free*. N.p., 2011. Web. Mar. 2011.

Lucado, Max. *Just Like Jesus: Learning to Have a Heart Like His.* Nashville, TN: Thomas Nelson, 2003. pg 3. Print.

Chapter 9
Reagan, Ronald. "Ronald Reagan Quotes." *Brainy Quote*. N.p., 2001. Web. Feb. 2011.

Jay, John. "Founding Father's Quotes. - Patriot Action Network." *Patriot Action Network*. N.p., n.d. Web. Feb. 2011.

Chapter 10
"Christian Quotes of the Founding Fathers." *About.com*. N.p., n.d. Web. Feb. 2011

Washington, George. "George Washington Quotes." *Brainy Quote*. N.p., 2001. Web. Feb. 2011.

Adams, Samuel. "Land of the Free - A Conservative Politics Web Site." *The Land of the Free*. N.p., 2011. Web. Mar. 2011.

"Christianity in America." *Faith of our Fathers*. N.p., n.d. Web. Feb. 2011.

Jefferson, Thomas. "Land of the Free - A Conservative Politics Web Site." *The Land of the Free*. N.p., 2011. Web. Mar. 2011.

Jefferson, Thomas. "Land of the Free - A Conservative Politics Web Site." *The Land of the Free*. N.p., 2011. Web. Mar. 2011.

Franklin, Benjamin. "Land of the Free - A Conservative Politics Web Site." *The Land of the Free*. N.p., 2011. Web. Mar. 2011.

Jefferson, Thomas. *Founders' Quotes.* N.p., 2011. Web. Feb. 2011

Jefferson, Thomas. "Thomas Jefferson Quotes." *Brainy Quote.* N.p., 2001. Web. Feb. 2011.

Jefferson, Thomas. "Thomas Jefferson Quotes." *Brainy Quote.* N.p., 2001. Web. Feb. 2011.

Jackson, Alan. "Small Town Southern Man". <u>Good Times</u>. Arista Nashville, 2007.

Chapter 11

Fairchild, Mary. "Christian Quotes of the Founding Fathers." *About.com.* N.p., n.d. Web. Feb. 2011.

Rogers, Adrian. *Ten Secrets for a Successful Family.* Wheaton, IL: Crossway Books, 1996. 138. Print

Chapter 12

"Chief Justice Richard Storey on Religion and Liberty." *First Amendment Religion Clauses.* Churchvstate, 20 June 2008. Web. Feb 2011.

Adams, John. "John Adams Quotes." *Brainy Quote.* N.p., 2001. Web. Feb. 2011.

Jefferson, Thomas. *Founders' Quotes.* N.p., 2011. Web. Feb. 2011

Jay, John. *Founders' Quotes.* N.p., 2011. Web. Feb. 2011

Webster, Daniel. "Christian Quotes." *Buzzle.* N.p. 2011. Web. May, 2011.

Adams, John. "John Adams Quotes." *Brainy Quote.* N.p., 2001. Web. Feb. 2011.

Chapter 13
Jefferson, Thomas. "Land of the Free - A Conservative Politics Web Site." *The Land of the Free*. N.p., 2011. Web. Mar. 2011.

Chapter 14
Adams, Samuel. "Land of the Free - A Conservative Politics Web Site." *The Land of the Free*. N.p., 2011. Web. Mar. 2011.

Chapter 15
Washington, George. "Land of the Free - A Conservative Politics Web Site." *The Land of the Free*. N.p., 2011. Web. Mar. 2011.

Hogg. RS., Strathdee, SA., Craib, KJP., O'Shaughnessy, MV., Montainer, JSG., Schechter, MT. " Modeling the Impact of HIV Disease on Mortality in Gay and Bisexual Men." *International Journal of Epidemiology,* Vol. 26, No. 3, 1997, pp. 657-61. Web. May 2011.

CPSIA information can be obtained at www.ICGtesting.com
Printed in the USA
241771LV00002B/2/P

9 781613 795026